BASIC GAME
DESIGN AND CREATION
FOR FUN & LEARNING

BASIC GAME DESIGN AND CREATION FOR FUN & LEARNING

NANU SWAMY
NAVEENA SWAMY

CHARLES RIVER MEDIA
Hingham, Massachusetts

Cover Design: Tyler Creative

Charles River Media
25 Thomson Place
Boston, Massachusetts 02210
617-757-7900
617-757-7969 (FAX)
info@charlesriver.com
www.charlesriver.com

This book is printed on acid-free paper.

Nanu Swamy and Naveena Swamy. *Basic Game Design and Creation for Fun & Learning.*
ISBN: 1-58450-446-3

Library of Congress Cataloging-in-Publication Data
Swamy, Nanu.
  Basic game design & creation / Nanu Swamy and Naveena Swamy.
    p. cm.
  Includes index.
  ISBN 1-58450-446-3 (pbk. with cd : alk. paper)
  1. Computer games--Design. 2. Object-oriented methods (Computer
science) I. Title: Basic game design and creation. II. Swamy, Naveena.
III. Title.
  QA76.76.C672S77 2006
  794.8'1536--dc22
                    2005031860

Printed in the United States of America
06 7 6 5 4 3 2 First Edition

Contents

Acknowledgments

This book has been made possible due to the extraordinary efforts of several people. We'd like to first thank David Pallai and Jennifer Niles for their interest in publishing the content we have created over the last four years since the founding of RoboTech Center. We'd like to also thank Mark Overmars, the creator of the *Game Maker* software, who has provided an easy path for game enthusiasts to create their own games.

The material in this book has been created from the voluminous material collected over many years while teaching several hundred game enthusiasts 2D and 3D game design programs at the RoboTech Center (*http://www.robotechcenter.com*). We'd like to thank all the participants for providing valuable feedback. We'd like to thank our student Collin Smith for his ideas and enthusiasm for Game Design.

Stephanie Nunn did an incredible job browsing through the preliminary document and providing valuable insight. Deepa did a great job trying out the examples and found it to be fun and entertaining. No words can describe the deepest appreciation we have for our daughter, Ramya, and our son, Rohit, whose excitement and enthusiasm for game design gave us all the energy we needed in helping us create this manuscript. And finally we'd like to thank Jennifer Blaney for all her assistance during the preparation of the manuscript and Bryan Davidson for his help during the production process.

Foreword

Computer games have become an important form of entertainment. People of all ages, both men and women, play computer games. People play games on their PCs, consoles, handheld devices and mobile phones. They play many different types of games. Shooters, adventure games, role-playing games, puzzle games, etc. And the interest in gaming is expected to increase even further over the coming years.

Playing games is a lot of fun. But creating games can be even more fun. When you create a game, you determine the rules of the game. You decide on the graphics and the sound effects. You make up the story line. And you create the levels and the puzzles. Once the game is ready you can give it to your friends to play and enjoy!

Creating commercial quality computer games is clearly something that is not easy to do. Budgets for commercial games nowadays are many millions of dollars and are created by large teams of specialists. But you don't need all this to make simple and interesting games. Also you do not need to be a programmer. The *Game Maker* package developed by me enables you to create your games without writing a line of code. And this book teaches you how to do it without writing any software code or scripts.

This book provides a jumpstart for creating games without the use of complex software scripts or code. *Game Maker* has a very active user community (check out the forums at *http://forums.gamemaker.nl/*). Create games with the program and share these with others and take part in this active forum of avid game designers

Game Maker is also an excellent education tool. It is used all over the world in all levels of education, ranging from schools to universities. Creating games challenges students to think logical and abstract, while at the same moment encourages them to be creative. Game design is a confluence of varied streams of technology like Computer Science, Arts, Physics and Mathematics.

Game Maker uses an object-oriented approach. All characters, items, explosions, etc. are modeled as objects. Objects react to events by performing certain actions. This event-driven object-oriented mechanism is common to most modern programming languages. Users of *Game Maker* learn to think in such a way without even noticing, and without the need to learn a programming language.

But, besides the educational benefits, creating computer games is simply a lot of fun. Entering the world of game design will be the beginning of a fascinating journey. This book is dedicated to inspire aspiring game designers and will help you take the first steps. Enjoy the ride.

Mark Overmars
Creator of *Game Maker*
http://www.gamemaker.nl/

Introduction

Millions of people play video games. This book is created for those who want to go a step further and create their own games. It is designed to lay the foundation for game enthusiasts interested in embarking on a journey that will transform them from being passive game players into creative game designers!

This book is an attempt to break the myth that one needs in-depth skills in computer science and digital art to create interactive computer games. As you go through this book, you will appreciate that a basic understanding of computers—knowledge of the use of a mouse and a keyboard—is all that you need to get started on creating simple games. The book portrays two different, but interconnected, technologies. The first is game design, which teaches game enthusiasts simple techniques to create games, and the second is object technology, a new and natural paradigm for creating software that is revolutionizing the software industry.

In this book we refrain from building games that belong to the category of violent "shoot-em-up" games found in abundance on the market today. Instead, we focus on more eductional games that groups of game enthusiasts are working on known as serious games. These educational games can stimulate game players into thinking and learning concepts using new pedagogical paradigms in fun and interesting ways. Included in this book is an example of such a game called *The DNA Factory*. It is a simple game that requires the player to pair proteins together and synthesize DNA. Another game is called *Bug Invasion*, which involves the extermination of various types of insects. Both of these games have great educational value.

The content of the book is designed to lay a foundation for an introduction to object-oriented game development. It uses engaging exercises that introduce you to game design, object-oriented paradigms, software design, software development, and product testing.

The book enables audiences with diverse backgrounds in areas such as music, liberal arts, education, medicine, science, and technology to create a rich tapestry of games incorporating various concepts from their fields. Every chapter introduces new concepts with detailed examples to guide you into becoming a serious game designer.

We have always felt that technical books must be easy to read. People learn by analogies, and anything that is abstract can be hard for the untrained mind to understand. In this book, we explain game design by creating objects and analogies that exist in the real world. This, we believe, makes our book to be as easy to read as a storybook.

GAME DESIGN AND PLANNING

This book demystifies the complex process of game design in an easy-to-follow, step-by-step format that includes reference figures and sample demonstrations that make the game design process fun and effective. It also allows you to progress quickly and take an idea from concept into a fully playable game. Whether or not you are looking at game creation for fun or learning, you'll find out how to make your own games. So, let's begin our journey in learning how to make and design games the easy way.

You're probably itching to make your first game and just get on with it. That's not all bad, as it's good to be enthusiastic about a subject you are involved in (it will be a major benefit later). However, let's ask a simple question: "How many people do you think buy a new game and then proceed to read the enclosed instruction manual?" Many people who play games usually just install them and start playing. The problem with not reading the manual is that while you do learn when you're playing, you are likely to lose the first few games you play because you don't understand all the underlying things you need to do. It all seems easy enough when you first start playing the game, but you soon get out of your depth and have to start looking through the manual to find the answers. If we take this approach to making games, the same theory applies, but there are obvious pitfalls. Why design a game (which could take some time) when you can just come up with the idea quickly, make it, and then send it to friends? To some extent, there is no problem with just going off and creating a game idea, especially if it's just for fun. If you are going to take up the challenge of a larger project, you will find that if you consider making a change to the underlying game (or it doesn't work quite as you imagined), you may have to rewrite large portions of the program. Without some form of planning, you could be wasting a lot of time and effort and increasing the overall development time of your game. Even if you're just making a game for fun, you still need to figure out what the goal of your game is going to be and what types of components will be included.

WHY CREATE GAMES?

You may have many reasons to make games, and using Game Maker is a great way to achieve many of them. Some reasons you want to make games may include:

- You want a job in the games industry.
- You wish to sell your own games.
- You want to get your game published and sold by someone else.
- You wish to make games as a hobby.
- Perhaps you are bored of playing games and you want to make your own, as you feel you might be able to do better.
- You want to make games for your friends and family.
- You are a teacher looking at getting your students to learn useful skills such as story telling, mathematics, art, and design while keeping them interested in the lesson.

As you can see, there are many reasons to make games (this list isn't definitive), but whatever your reason, it is important to ensure you enjoy the experience.

BASIC GAME DESIGN AND PLANNING

What do you need to do, and in what order, to make sure your idea is a success? There are no right or wrong answers to that question, so this book simply points you in the right direction and gives you some ideas to try.

The Ideas

So, you have an idea; in fact, you are likely to have more than one. Which one would you choose and start to put a lot of time and effort into? Even a small project will require that you to invest some time and effort in the game design—even the tiny games you might make for the Internet or free download.

You may have many good ideas, but you have to be objective and realize that you cannot implement them all at once. The best way to do this is to complete a simple table of game ideas, as shown in Table I.1.

TABLE I.1

Game Type	Idea	Technology Concept	Rating	Difficulty
Car Racing	You are a budding race car driver wanting to become a race champion. Before you can complete in the world championship, you need to win the regional heats.	Top-down scrolling	High	Medium
Flight SIM	You are a WWI pilot who has just joined your squadron and must take to the skies as soon as you arrive.	Story-driven 3D flight SIM	Medium	High (impossible?)
Scrolling	Aliens have invaded a small town in your area. A band of citizens cannot simply stand by and watch the impending disaster. A small team armed with weapons goes in search of the alien menace.	Isometric scrolling	Low	Medium

Using Table I.1, set out all your current game ideas; even if it's a silly or half-thought-out concept, write it down. Ideas shouldn't be judged at this point, so it's a good idea to keep notes of all game ideas in one place. The purpose of this table is to begin to reduce our ideas to a select few; that way, we can make inroads into what we really want to make.

The table is then split it into five columns. Although the table is simplistic, we don't want to get into any detail at this stage. In fact, we want to keep it simple and not write too much; later, we will expand on the ideas of those games that deserve more time and effort.

The columns are separated as follows:

Type: Categorize the game type into one of the standard gaming groups, for example, RPG, war game, flight simulation, isometric, fist-person shooter (FPS), etc.

Idea: A brief overview of what the game is about; at this stage, we are keeping it simple. A quick overview of the story and the aim of the game is all that is required.

Technology: What game technology will the game use? This could be top-down scrolling, side scrolling, 3D FPS, etc. This step is to give you an idea of what might be required from the tool you intend to use to make your game. It's not a good idea to make a 3D FPS if the product you're choosing can only make 2D games.

Rating: How high do you rate your idea? How excited are you at the prospect of making this game? If it's a low rating, it's not worth spending time and effort to make, as you will probably get bored and give up. We want you to be happy after completing your first game and ready to plunge into your next game project.

Difficulty: It's time to be honest about your skills with your chosen game-making product. Many people on game-making forums have never used a game-making product and want to make an online role-playing game or something similar that is just too complex. If you really think the game idea is too difficult, put it aside, as you don't want to start a project and then struggle with the concepts. This is meant to make your life easier and not deceive yourself into thinking you can make anything you want. There is no shame in admitting that an idea at this stage is too difficult, because later it might not be, and you'll have the idea on paper.

After you have reviewed the table and found the highest-rating game that strikes you as the most interesting (there may be more than one), you are ready to continue. However, before you get all excited and start making the game, you need to make sure the game-making tool is capable of carrying out your idea. Remember to use the "difficulty" column to decide between multiple high-rating game ideas.

Tool Choice

You have the game you want to make reduced to a few choice game ideas, or perhaps just one. Before you rush off and start it, take a few minutes to check that your ideas are compatible with the game-making tool you are using. In this book, we are going to be using Game Maker, which is specifically for 2D games; therefore, if you selected a 3D first person shooter, this wouldn't be the right tool for the job. It is very important that you understand both your own capabilities and those of the tools you are going to use.

Investigate your product choice thoroughly before starting any project. This includes knowing what any compiled program created with it runs on and any other specifications that might affect your decision, including what machines the final program will run on and any licensing rules regarding distribution.

The Story

It is very difficult to be unique with regard to stories these days, as many things have already been tried. Your story doesn't have to be unique or new—as long as the idea is well presented, and it's what you want to do. Spend some time writing your story, as this is the key to what will be included in your game. During real game design, the story is sketched out so that everyone can see what it is going to look like. This is called the *story plan* or *storyboard*, which is a simple document detailing some of the key elements of the story and what it will contain (it doesn't go into too much detail, as it's just trying to bring out the flavor of the story).

At this point, don't go into major detail, as it's just a scoping exercise to make sure you have an idea you ultimately like. You might find that once you have done this, you no longer like the idea and don't want to make it. If that's the case, you have succeeded, because no one should make games he or she doesn't want to make.

Screen Design

After completing the story, you need to understand how the game is going to look, which will give you an idea of how each screen or level will appear. This allows you to cast a designer's eye over the recommended structure and ensures that everything works correctly from a usability and layout point of view. If someone else will be making your graphics (this isn't uncommon), the screen design is also for his benefit, so you should create the designs the way you want them to look and then send them off to the graphic artist to generate.

Graphics

Only a small percentage of people can make good-looking graphics and animation. If you are one of the few, that's great, and it will be very helpful when you design your game layout and graphics to be used in the game. If you are not, you will run into some issues, so here are some ideas of where you might be able to get material for your programs.

You can choose from a number of options when looking for graphics:

Graphics libraries: A few graphics libraries are available on the Internet, some of which are free to use, while others have options to purchase. Again, make sure you read the small print on the Web sites, as some sites say that if you sell or distribute over 10,000 items of any one product, you will need a different license agreement. You may not want to worry about this right now, but you still should consider it, as you don't want to have to pull your product off the Internet or a CD because you cannot afford the licensing fees. Make sure you know what costs are involved before you start; that way, nothing will be a shock to you when and if you get past those levels. There are a few graphics CD-ROMs available on the market, but most of them are either clip art (which is no good for what we want to do) or very specialized.

Make your own: You may be a good enough artist and have the right tools for the job. If you decide to make your own graphics, consider the impact this might have on the time involved in making your game. This will definitely have a bearing on whether you have the time, effort, and patience to complete the project, as making graphics can be very time consuming.

Get someone else to make them: One of the challenges of making a game is to get help from other people, especially people you have never met. If you can find a graphic artist to help, make sure you understand how he works, and come to an agreement on time frame. Most graphic artists won't accept work unless there is some form of demo or game in existence. Don't try to get help when you have only written the story, as many artists won't bother to reply to the requests for help at that point. They need to know that you are serious about the project before putting their own time and effort into it.

Sound and Music

Very much a secondary thought in game creation, but still an important aspect to consider, is the sound and music you are going to have in your game. Although it may seem not as important as the graphics or game play, think about watching a movie without sound. Your overall opinion of the film would definitely go down. Sound and music give a game atmosphere, and that makes it appear more professional, if done correctly. The problem with sound and music is that they have the same problems that come with graphic creation: most people can't make their own and need to find someone or something to supply them.

Sound libraries: Do not to rush out to the local computer store and buy a music recording CD-ROM. These CD-ROMs are usually very poor quality and not very useful, even if they are cheap. There are a number of excellent professional Web sites you can visit to listen to and purchase and download a range of sounds and songs. Although you are going to have to spend money, you will be able to pick the exact sounds you want in your game. Conversely, if you purchase a cheap sound CD-ROM, you will have to browse the entire program looking for something that fits your needs. Moreover, you may find that there is nothing on it you would want to use and that the quality isn't high enough for what you want. Always read any licensing text off the Web site concerning using sounds commercially; most are okay, but read the small print to make sure.

Make your own: A few years ago, this would not have been practical unless you had some form of sound equipment (MIDI) and a talent in music creation. Today, however, a number of products are available that can help you make music and sounds relatively easily.

Get someone else to make them: The same issues exist with outsourcing graphics apply here; make sure you have a specific time frame for completing the work.

GAME TYPES

Before looking at how to develop and design our own games, let's take a quick look at the various game types that you as a developer might want to make and what people would like to play.

This is always a good place to start, as each game can be categorized, and you will then find it easier to think about which type you would enjoy making. (Enjoying the game-making process is very important for your overall sanity and making sure your enthusiasm is kept high for a project.) Again, this list isn't definitive but it includes most of the game types you might be considering for your next project. This book is all about making 2D games and does not touch on 3D game creation aspects.

If you are interested in learning more about 3D programming or development, you can read the Charles River Media books Elementary Game Programming & Simulators Using Jamagic *by Sergio Perez, or* Awesome 3D Game Development: No Programming Required *by Clayton E Crooks II.*

Platform Games

Most game players at some point have probably played a 2D platform game. They are not premium titles at stores, as was the case some time ago, but they are still very popular. 3D platform games are more popular on console machines and PC's. From a retro gaming point of view, they are still as popular as ever (if not more so), as many games from that period were crafted cleverly to overcome the hardware constraints by introducing a nice game play.

You can still find 2D platform games as popular free downloads or games available to play directly from a Web site (as a marketing or sales tool); therefore, it is a great type of game to pick. With platform games, you have to take into account ladders, drops and falls, escalators, and elevators. Although this isn't a beginner's subject matter, it is not too difficult to do once you understand some basic concepts. We look at how to make platform games later in the book.

Scrolling Shooters

This was a popular type of game in the 1980s and it's still a popular format of game for retro game makers. Shoot-'em-up games would normally have the gamer playing a space fighter pilot defending the Earth against wave after wave of alien invaders. The game could scroll from left to right or bottom to top and could include bonuses for destroying a wave of enemy fighters, including shield and weapons up-grades—very predictable stuff, but entertaining all the same. These types of games are relatively easy to create; in fact, once you have done the scrolling, most of the hard work is done (except for having some original graphics, of course).

Board Games

Chess and solitaire are just two examples of traditional board games that have been converted to the computer game for-mat. They have a niche following with a specific part of the market, and this type of game seems to appear in large num-bers on many budget labels. Board games are certainly not difficult to make with regard to the graphics side; the chal-lenge you will face is with the computer artificial intelligence (AI) responding to the player's moves. Computer AI is com-plex and certainly more difficult to design and program, so you shouldn't attempt board games when just starting out.

Card Games

Another popular format on budget labels is card games. A card game is a great time filler, so when you have a few min-utes to spare, usually it's one of the first games to be loaded up. A very good reason for wanting to make card games is that they don't normally need a powerful computer or com-plex graphics to run.

Another plus of picking a card game to make is that there are many types from which to choose. You could also make memory games using your card graphics set, as this is an-other simple, straightforward concept. Therefore, you won't have difficulty finding something you would be comfortable attempting to make; all you need is one set of card graphics and your game idea, and you are set.

Racing Games

One popular type of game on the Commodore Amiga® was the top-down view race car game. Various tracks, bonuses, and great computer AI would make for an exciting and increasingly difficult set of race tracks. The great thing about race car games is that you can add so much to the game, and it's easy to think of new and interesting ideas for it. When considering what type of game you are going to make, consider a type of game from which ideas flow easily. If you are struggling for ideas early in your game creation, it may be better to pick another game type—you can always come back to your original game idea later if you have some more ideas to add to it. Car racing games are not the easiest to create from a graphics generation point of view, but you certainly won't be stuck for ideas. Car games could have weapons to destroy other cars, weather conditions, car upgrades to make them faster, single races, or tournaments. The main things you will need to consider when making this type of game are the graphics and the computer AI.

Bat and Ball Games

A very popular type of game on the early 8-bit and 16-bit computers was the bat and ball style of games. You usually control a paddle and have to destroy blocks using a bouncing ball. There have been various variations of this type of game over the years in which several things have changed: the direction of the paddle and balls, various positive and negative effects when destroying certain blocks, and even 3D versions. There many options for improving and adding new features, and you shouldn't have too many problems thinking up new ideas.

WHAT IS A DESIGN DOCUMENT?

A design document is often overlooked in the rush and excitement of a game idea. After all, if you have a unique idea that could conceivably be a great game, why would you want to waste your time working on something that doesn't really get you any closer to the end product?

Many times, even relatively large development teams don't spend the time to create a fully functional design document. Most game developers will try to stay away from unnecessary work, but the long hours spent creating a thorough design document actually save countless hours later down the development road. You might be lucky enough to create a very good game without a design document, but the key word in this is luck. Most often, a game that begins without a properly developed design document will be delayed for months or may not even be finished.

A design document is similar to a movie script. In it, you will write details of an exact story (if you have one—for example, racing games would probably not have a story), an overview of the characters or opponents you are intending to create, detailed descriptions of every level, and so on. If this is the first time you've ever considered creating a design document, you should be aware of a few things.

First, the design document is not chiseled into stone. That is, it can and should evolve as the game does, but it shouldn't be drastically altered. The design document will serve as a sort of road map to how the project will develop and should be as complete as possible. That being said, it can be changed when necessary to include a new character or a slight change in the plot. Design documents are team oriented and therefore should include as many contributions as possible from the individuals who make up a team.

A design document is important for a number of reasons. To a potential publisher, it details the game and shows them a vision of what you are hoping to accomplish. The purpose of a design document to a team is rather simple: it lays out the responsibilities of everyone involved. Depending on the team member, a design document will mean different things.

It is the document from which a producer will base their estimates, while programmers may look at the design document as series of instructions for completing their roles. Artists will use the document to help them visualize the characters they need to create. Designers often take things from the document such as the mood for a level. Audio personnel require some sort of a basis for the development of sound effects and music, and the document may be the only place they can acquire the appropriate knowledge.

ELEMENTS OF THE DESIGN DOCUMENT

Lets look at the individual components of a design document. Many teams will include information such as legal issues, target audience, and market analysis for a game in their design document. While this works, it would make sense to include those types of business materials in a game proposal to a publisher. It's counterproductive to have team members scrolling through pages of information they really don't need to review.

Game Overview (Storyline)

This may be the most important piece of the document. Without a solid story or game overview, the later steps will be much more difficult to create. Be very thorough with the game overview. If you realize you left something out, go back and fix it immediately. Sometimes the smallest details can make a big difference in a large project.

Because you don't know exactly who will read the game overview, make sure to use as many details as possible, as you would if you were creating a good storybook. You would be surprised at the number of simple spelling errors in most design documents. While everyone misses a word every now and then, you should try your best to keep grammar and spelling mistakes to a minimum. This is not directly important to you, but again, you don't know who might end up reading your design document.

Many teams place background information in its own category, but because it relates to the story, it can be placed within the game overview category. Some genres, such as a sports simulation, wouldn't have a background section and can therefore be passed over.

Levels

The next item you need to address is the levels that make up a game. If you do a thorough job in the preceding step, this one is very easy. Compile a list of levels, in the order in which they will be encountered in your game, adding any details you deem necessary. Optional materials include ideas such as the layout and a general description or the placement of enemies. Creating a mood for a level at this time can be a big bonus, as a designer or artist can simply browse this area to get a feel for what needs to be created.

The creation of a set of maps for the levels is helpful to the members of the team—especially the programmers and level designers. They can be very detailed pictures but more likely will be a set of simple lines, circles, and squares that form a rough layout of the levels.

Heroes and Enemies

The next section of the design document deals with the characters that will be included in your game. Like the level area of the document, the character section should fall into place if the game overview is meticulous.

Most game have two basic types of characters: heros and enemies. You can include details of the hero such as background information or rough sketches. These ideas will again help team members understand what you want to accomplish. A list and description of animations should be included with every hero as well. Depending on their roles in the story, you can also include descriptive ideas of their intelligence level and strength and basic information about how they react to the other characters. Again, this information will be beneficial to the team.

Once you finish with the heroes, you need to create a section for the enemies you will encounter. This could include anything that will attack a player. For instance, you might include a dinosaur or in a space combat game, you could include an asteroid. You can follow the same basic procedures as you did for the characters, making sure to include similar details and sketches where appropriate.

Last, you need to include information about the types of weapons the characters will have access to. You should include detailed descriptions of every weapon that can be accessed by both types of character. Sketches can be valuable for everyone on the team. You should create a list that contains the damage the weapons will create along with they type and amount of ammunition.

You can make sketches as detailed or as simple as you need based on your particular needs. Often, it's more important to get them drawn than to worry about how great they look. You can always go back and clean them up later.

Audio Effects

This section is important to the audio personnel on the team and the programmers who will be using their sounds in the game. You can discuss the possibilities of tools that you plan to employ and the types of sound effects that you have in mind and possibly detail the music you might have in the levels that you listed earlier in the document.

The most important step in the first draft of the document is to include what formats and sound API (application programming interface) you are planning to use and what types of music and sound effects you are planning. For instance, you should decide if you are going to use MIDI, WAV, or MP3 files for the music and if you'll need sound effects such as explosions or footsteps. You should also list the genres of music you'll be planning, for example, rock or pop. This keeps the programmers and audio personnel thinking the same way so that they are not surprised two months into the project.

Single Player or Multiplayer

The next step focuses on the game play itself. If you worked hard on the game overview, you may have already covered this and this section will be much easier. If not, you should begin by determining if the game will implement single player, multiplayer, or both. For example, if you are planning a clone like Quake, you might decide that it is single player only. If you are doing a sports game like basketball, you'll probably want to have multiple player support. Sometimes the information in this area of the document is discussed in other areas, but you shouldn't worry about duplication of ideas. This is especially true on a first draft, as you can always change the document after a later inspection.

If it's a single player game, you can describe the game experience in a few sentences and perhaps break down some of the key elements of the game. For example, if it's a Quake clone, you could begin by setting up the location of the game. Next, you could detail the types of enemies you'll be facing and the route to complete the game, that is, you have to finish 10 levels before the game is over. You could also list how the game ends, for instance, if you don't complete the level on time. Another idea you can include is a projection of the number of hours the game is going to take before a player finishes and how the player ultimately wins the game. A single-player game is usually easier not only to design but also to discuss in the design document.

A multiplayer game description begins the same way as a single-player game. You can take a few sentences to describe the basics of the game play. A basketball game description could begin with a mention of the type of game it is. For example, if it is a street ball type of game, college, professional, or international rules game. You can also decide what types of options you'll have, such as franchise mode for a professional game, or what types of parks you'll include for a street ball game. For complex games this is a good time to decide how many players will be allowed to play simultaneously and how you plan to implement the client-server or peer-to-peer system. For instance, do you plan to use something like DirectPlay or another API, and how many individuals do you plan to allow to play against one another. In the basketball example, you need to decide how many people you will allow to play on the same team or against one another on different teams. You don't need to have complete technical details, but you should at least discuss the possibility of the protocol you plan to use. It would be even better to begin looking at potential pitfalls that are common in multiplayer games.

SUMMARY

Take some time to plan and design your project. This ensures that you stay within your development time and budget (if any). If you are creating a small game, the process doesn't have to be as intense or in-depth as some of the suggestions made here; these are only recommendations, and you can amend them to suit your way of working.

Remember, we all have different success levels; for example, if your plan is to make your game fun and enjoyable for friends and family, that's your success criteria. But these concepts will help you even if you are creating games for a small audience, so don't think you need a big plan to put some structure into what you are making. Use a common sense approach to game design and creation, and enjoy the process.

CHAPTER 1

Software Installation

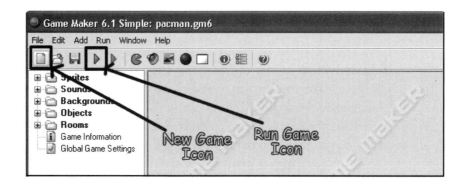

In this chapter:

- Game Maker Installation Procedure
- Testing the Install
- Loading a Game
- Playing the Game

Many tools of varying complexity are available for creating games. Some require knowledge of programming languages such as C++ or Java or scripting languages such as JavaScript. Other tools make it easy for people to create simple games by assembling several lines of code into functional units that are represented by variety of icons that describe the behavior of the functional component. These icons define specific functional characteristics that game objects can perform. Icons are typically dragged into a sequential array of blocks that define a behavior. Game Maker® is an icon-based, drag-and-drop game design tool. In this chapter, we are going to explain the steps necessary to install the Game Maker software required for creating games described in this book. We are eager to get you started in designing your own games in the easiest possible way.

Manufacturing industries use the just-in-time concept, in which the correct quantity of raw materials is brought in for assembly just when it is required. We use the just-in-time concept throughout the book to provide you with the right amount of information you will need to understand the game creation process. Too much unnecessary information can lead to information overload. As you progress, you will appreciate the fact that an in-depth knowledge of computer science or digital art is not a prerequisite to create games using Game Maker.

We will begin by loading and running a sample game and then progressing to create our own games in subsequent chapters.

GAME MAKER INSTALLATION PROCEDURE

Insert the CD-ROM that came with this book into your computer's CD-ROM drive. The CD-ROM contains the Game Maker software, several example games, a library of sprites, and some tutorials explained in the form of a video. Once your computer has successfully read the CD-ROM, you may automatically see a window similar to the one shown in Figure 1.1 that provides you with an opportunity to display all of the files available on the CD-ROM. You could press the OK button of this window to view your files.

If your computer does not automatically start up a window like that shown in Figure 1.1, click on the MyComputer icon (Figure 1.2) or Windows Explorer (Figure 1.3) on your desktop.

FIGURE 1.1 The View Files window.

FIGURE 1.3   The
Windows Explorer icon.

FIGURE 1.2   The
MyComputer icon.

To start the installation, close all other applications and
double-click on the file gmaker.exe found in the Application
ON THE CD   directory of the CD-ROM. You should see the startup screen,
as shown in Figure 1.4.

FIGURE 1.4   Game Maker Installation startup screen.

Click on the Next button to continue with the installation. You will see the Game Maker Product Information box,

as shown in Figure 1.5. Browse through the information and then press the Next button to proceed.

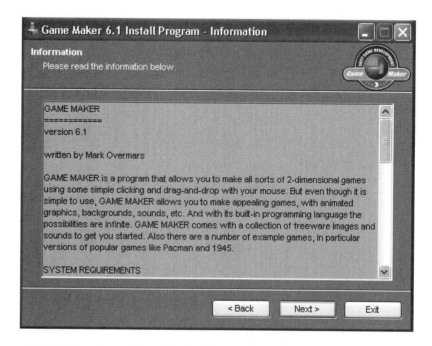

FIGURE 1.5   Game Maker Product Information window.

The next screen (Figure 1.6) is the Game Maker License Agreement. Read the agreement and conform to the licensing agreement by clicking on the radio button next to the statement "I agree with the above terms and conditions." Click on the Next button to proceed with the install.

The window shown in Figure 1.6 asks you to define the location where the software is to be installed on your machine. It may be best to leave the default location as is to make it easier to follow all of the instructions provided in later chapters. If you choose a different location, define the new location by typing it into the text box provided or use the browse button highlighted in Figure 1.7 to browse and select a location. Remember that the location you choose will be the location where examples, executables, and other Game Maker components can be found.

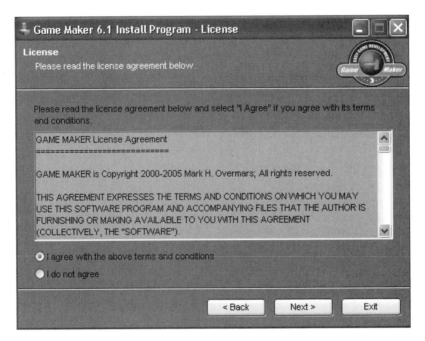

FIGURE 1.6   Game Maker License Agreement.

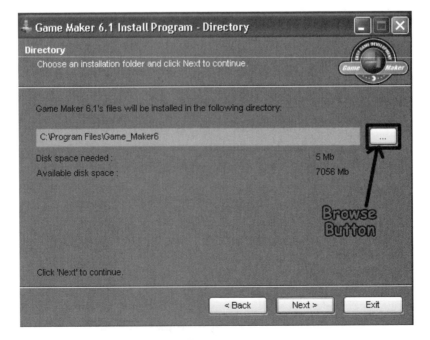

FIGURE 1.7   Game Maker Install Program Directory

After you are satisfied with the directory in which Game Maker will be installed, click on the Next button. You should then see a new screen, as shown in Figure 1.8.

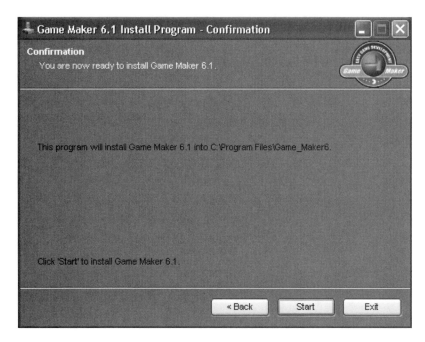

FIGURE 1.8   Game Maker Install Confirmation.

If you define a destination directory that does not exist, you will be prompted with a dialog box asking you to confirm the creation of the new directory. Press the Yes button to proceed.

Click on the Start button when you are ready. You should see installation steps being completed one-by-one and finally you should see the window shown in Figure 1.9. Your installation is now complete. We have the opportunity to test our software immediately after the installation. You are now given an opportunity to "Launch Game Maker 6.1." Make sure the box is checked as shown in Figure 1.9. Click on the Exit button to close this window. Game Maker should start up in a few moments. We are now ready to test our installation.

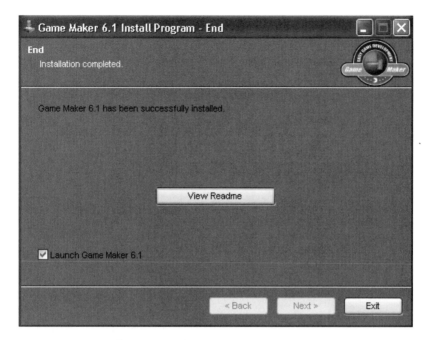

FIGURE 1.9   Installation Completion screen.

TESTING THE INSTALL

You should see the Game Maker startup screen, as shown in Figure 1.10. By default, Game Maker runs in the Advanced Mode. Let's change it to the Simple Mode by clicking on the menu item File > Advanced Mode. The Advanced menu option in the File menu should be unchecked to be in the Simple mode. Figure 1.11 shows the difference between the Simple and Advanced File menus. Let's make sure we are in the Simple Mode before we proceed further.

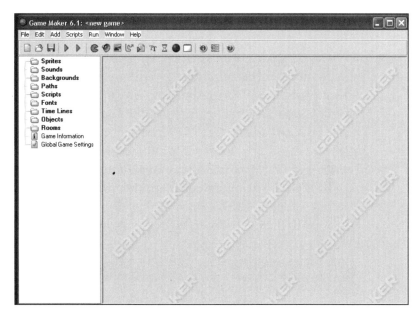

FIGURE 1.10   The Game Maker Startup screen.

FIGURE 1.11   The Simple and Advanced File Menus.

LOADING A GAME

Let's now load and run a sample game to make sure we have all the pieces installed perfectly. This will also help us check to see if we have all the underlying software libraries required to run Game Maker. For example, the Game Maker software uses the Microsoft DirectX® software libraries. If the sample game does not run, we need to update the software libraries before we attempt to create our own games.

To load the examples, click on the File menu item at the top left corner of the Game Maker window and click on Open from the drop-down menu, as shown in Figure 1.12.

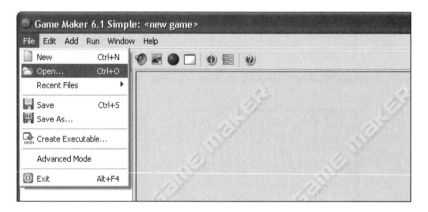

FIGURE 1.12   Loading Game Maker game files.

ON THE CD

You should be automatically prompted with a list of Game Maker example files that have been automatically installed for you at the installation location—C:\Program files\GameMaker_6\Examples if you used the default location. Several examples are listed as shown in Figure 1.13. Let's choose the game *Pacman* to start with. Click on Pacman and then click on the Open button. You should see a Game Loading Progression bar flash momentarily on the screen. After that, the *Pacman* game and its resources appear (Figure 1.14).

FIGURE 1.13   List of examples.

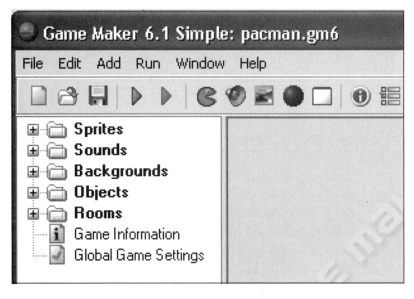

FIGURE 1.14   *Pacman* game with resources loaded.

Note that the name *Pacman* is displayed on the top left corner of the window as pacman.gm6. As a small exercise to become familiar with the user interface, place your cursor over each of the small icons below the main menu bar. A menu-tip help item should provide you with an indication of what each icon is used for. For example, if you place your mouse over the first icon (Figure 1.15), a textbox informs you that this icon is used to "create a new game file."

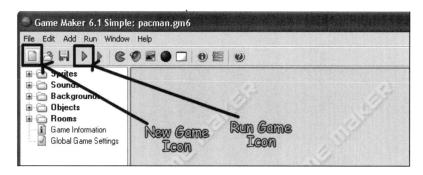

FIGURE 1.15 Create Game and Run Game icons.

It is a good idea to spend a few minutes and visit each icon. This will give you an idea of some of the things you can do with Game Maker.

PLAYING THE GAME

Let's play *Pacman*. There are several ways to run the game we have loaded. We will show you the easiest way first. To run the game click on the Run button represented by the green arrow icon shown in Figure 1.15.

The game should be loaded and should start running after you press the green arrow button. In this game, you control Pacman, who is represented by the red smiley face. The cursor keys move Pacman in different directions. For more detailed playing instructions, press the F1 key on your keyboard. A pop-up screen will appear, providing you with the information about the game, the rules, and the keys used to play the game. This help feature is very helpful to incorporate into any game you create.

To quit or end the game, press the Escape key on your keyboard. Now that you have played the game, you may want to investigate a portion of the user interface by clicking on the + symbols to the left of some of the resources. This expands the resource tree. For example, you could click on the + button to the left of the sprites resource, as shown in Figure 1.14. If you recursively expand all the + buttons beneath the one you last expanded, you will get a complete list of all the sprites that are used in the *Pacman* game.

Now that you have played a game on Game Maker, let's get ready to create our own.

SUMMARY

In this chapter, we installed the Game Maker software, our icon-based, drag-and-drop game design tool. We tested our installation by loading a sample game and playing it, and learned the controls for selecting a game file, playing a game, and ending a game. There are a few more examples that we will explore in the following chapters: *1945.gm6* is a game similar to *Space Invaders*, there is a car racing game named *streetrace.gm6*.

CHAPTER 2

Game Creation

OBJECTS-Actions & Events : A Robot

Event: If collision with wall

Action: Back up and move away.

In this chapter:

- What are Objects?
- Creating Our First Game
- Loading Sprites
- Creating Objects
- Creating Game Rooms
- Object Lifecycle
- Adding Events
- Adding Actions
- Adding a Collision Event
- Adding Score
- Playing the Game

Now that the installation has been completed successfully, we are ready to start creating games. Designing games is something that anyone can learn to successfully do. The two key elements required for creating games are digital art and computer logic. These two fields are quite distinct, and it is difficult to find someone who is an expert in both. In the current world of education, one might specialize in either digital art or computer logic to attain a graduate degree, but only a handful of colleges have programs specializing in the field of game design, which is an amalgamation of computer software and digital art.

In this book, we will be using tools that soften the complexity of the game design process and provide the user with an easy to use interface that helps in the creation of games. The Game Maker software is our tool of choice for this book, for it encapsulates a lot of the complexity involved in creating games by using little blocks that we can move around to create different objects that behave differently. In computer science, we think of the world in terms of objects that contain behavior patterns condensed into common building blocks. This is called *object-oriented programming*, which is part of a much broader concept called *object technology*. Object technology provides a new programming paradigm that creates a fundamental change in the way we look at the world and develop new products.

WHAT ARE OBJECTS?

Before we start creating games, we need to understand the concept of objects. Take a moment to look around you. What do you see? Maybe there are computers, lights, pencils, pens, and erasers. Maybe there are desks, chairs, chalkboards, books, people, doors, and walls. If you are outdoors there may be trees, leaves, grass, birds, insects, and more. In the world of object technology all of these things are objects. We view the world as a set of independent objects that interact with each other, and each object has a set of behaviors that describes what it can do. If we restrict our thinking to a living object such as a mouse, for example, some of the things it can do are as follows:

- It can eat.
- It can run.
- It can squeak.
- It can hide.
- It can sense danger.

Depending on a wide range of conditions, the mouse can execute more complex actions that are combinations of simple actions. The actions it performs are triggered by different kinds of events. For example, when the mouse gets hungry, its brain triggers several events that make the mouse search for some food and then eat it. Figure 2.1 shows how a robot responds to external events.

OBJECTS-Actions & Events : *A Robot*

Event: If collision with wall
Action: Back up and move away.

FIGURE 2.1   Objects and actions. Images courtesy of Ramya Swamy. Reprinted with permission.

We could similarly visualize a piece of cheese as an object with a very limited set of behaviors. We could think of it as an object that disseminates a distinct "cheesy" odor. This cheesy scent can be smelled only from a limited distance, as shown in Figure 2.2. As the mouse gets closer to the cheese, the smell gets stronger and stronger.

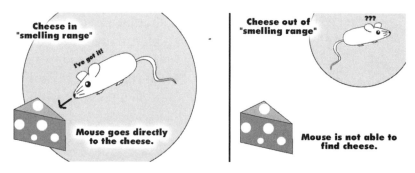

FIGURE 2.2   Cheese objects smell variance with distance. Images courtesy of Ramya Samy. Reprinted with permission.

What would happen if we take a real mouse and place it at a very far distance from the slice of cheese? The mouse will probably not even be aware that the cheese exists since it is not in its smelling range. It may eventually find the cheese accidently by running in a randomly chosen direction, but the chance of it finding the cheese is quite remote.

If we moved the cheese closer to the mouse, the mouse would immediately detect the scent of cheese in the air. It would sniff the air in two or three directions and then move in the direction that has the strongest scent of cheese. This is the algorithm that is programmed within its brain. What we are seeing here is the interaction of two objects in real life. One of them—the mouse—is a living object that can move. The other is a slice of cheese with a different set of characteristics.

When we create games, we use a similar algorithm. We first create a pictorial representation of the object and then attach certain behaviors to the object. If the object is a mouse, for example, we would draw a mouse using digital graphics software packages. Creating digital representations of real-world entities, by the way, is an industry of its own.

When creating a pictorial representation of an object, we have the option of drawing a two-dimensional (2D) digital representation of it or a three-dimensional (3D) version. A 2D digital picture can be thought of as a computerized version of a traditional sketch, such as a stick figure. A 3D digital picture can be thought of as a computerized version of a traditional sculpture, such as a clay pot. Many of today's animated movies, such as *Shrek* and *Finding Nemo*, use animated 3D models. In this book, we will be focusing on the use of 2D pictures to represent our objects. The 2D pictorial representation of an object is called a *sprite*.

CREATING OUR FIRST GAME

Our first game is going to be called ClickOnCash. In this game, there will be cash flying around in a room, and the goal is to grab as much cash as possible by clicking on it using the mouse. We will create a basic game first in order to understand the basic concepts of object-oriented game design.

Let's start Game Maker by clicking on the Game Maker icon (Figure 2.3) on your desktop or by navigating to it using the Windows Start button. If you are using the Windows Start button, look under the menu Start > All Programs > Game Maker 6 folder > Game Maker 6 program.

FIGURE 2.3   Game Maker
icon on your desktop.

Once you have Game Maker running, you should see the startup screen, as shown in Figure 2.4.

There are four main components in this startup screen: the Drop-Down Menu, the Main Toolbar, the Resource Explorer, and the Workspace. The Drop-Down Menu contains a list of operations you can perform by clicking on each drop-down menu item. This feature includes operations that will allow you to manipulate objects, read files, and so forth.

The Main Tool Bar has a list of picture icons you can use to perform different actions by clicking on them. Each of these icons has a help tool tip that displays a line of text when you place your cursor over the icon. This line of help text tells what the icon is used for.

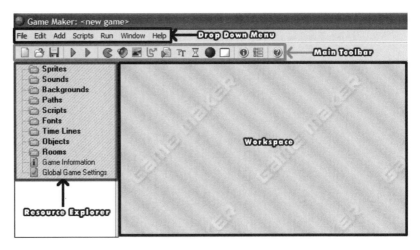

FIGURE 2.4   Game Maker startup screen with annotations.

The Resource Explorer window contains information about the resources you are using in your game. These resources are grouped into types such as sprites, sounds, backgrounds, objects, and rooms. This interface is similar to the Windows Explorer interface that allows you to browse through all the files on your computer. The Resource Explorer will have a + symbol before the group type name when there are resources of that particular kind being used. When you start up a fresh copy of Game Maker, no resources are loaded, so you will not see the + symbol.

The Workspace is the area where all of the resources are manipulated. Different context-sensitive dialog boxes open up in the workspace depending on the type of resource you are working on.

LOADING SPRITES

Sprites can be loaded by clicking on the Add Sprite icon (Figure 2.5) on the Main Toolbar. If you play around with the drop-down menu items, you may notice that there are many other ways to load a sprite. Let's load a sprite that will represent money in our game.

FIGURE 2.5   The Add Sprite
icon found on the Main Tool Bar.

Once you click on the Add Sprite icon, you will see the Sprite Properties dialog box open up (Figure 2.6) in the Workspace area. This dialog box provides you with an opportunity to change the properties of all the sprites that have been loaded.

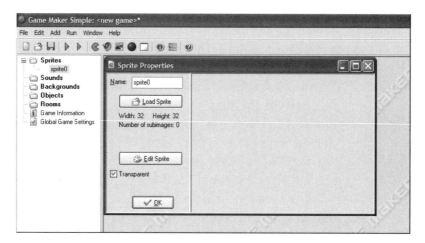

FIGURE 2.6   The Sprite Properties dialog box.

To load a sprite, click on the Load Sprite button. You will see the standard File Open dialog box. Navigate to the directory where Game Maker was installed. Click on the directory called Sprites and then on the directory called Various found beneath that. Choose the sprite named Money, as shown in Figure 2.7. Click on the Open button to complete the sprite load sequence.

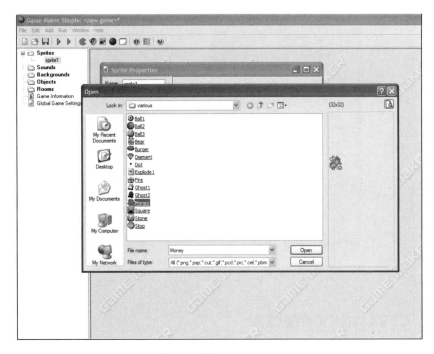

FIGURE 2.7   Load Sprite File Open box.

Now that the sprite is loaded, it is a good idea to change the default name of this sprite from sprite1 to cash, as shown in Figure 2.8, to avoid confusion. Click the OK button in the Sprite Properties dialog box to complete the sequence required to load a sprite.

Now, let's load a second sprite called square from the same location. Rename the sprite in the Sprites Properties box from sprite2 to wall, just as we did with the money sprite shown in Figure 2.8.

This completes the sprite loading sequence for our first game.

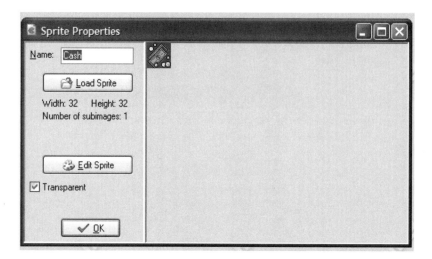

FIGURE 2.8   Sprite rename field.

CREATING OBJECTS

Sprites by themselves cannot be used in games. They do not exhibit any behavior and they do not have the intelligence to interact with their environment. In the next chapter, we will explain in detail what characteristics are required to create objects. For now it is sufficient to understand that objects can interact with events happening in the environment around them and can exhibit certain behaviors.

For example, when a mouse object sees an eagle object, the mouse object interacts with the proximity of the eagle object and tries to run away and hide as the eagle get closer. The closer the two objects are, the faster the mouse runs. Objects created in a game using Game Maker interact with each other just like objects interact in the real world.

Let's return for a moment to the mouse and cheese objects. If the mouse object sees a cheese object, what do you think the interaction would be? In all probability, the mouse would eat the cheese object, and then go to its nest and sleep. This is another case of two objects interacting with one another.

Now that we understand that objects can interact with events and exhibit different behaviors, let's look into how we can attach behaviors to objects.

To get started, click on the Add Object icon (Figure 2.9) on the Main Tool bar.

FIGURE 2.9   Add Object icon.

You should see the Workspace change. An Object Properties dialog box should show up, as shown in Figure 2.10.

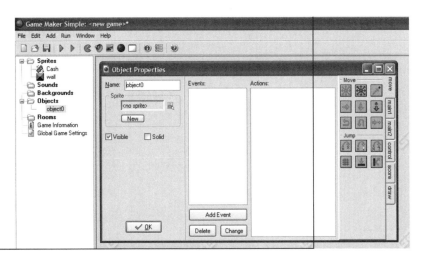

FIGURE 2.10   Object Properties dialog box.

This property box is where game objects are made alive. Let's rename the current object, object0, a more meaningful name such as CashObject. To do this, click on the textbox next to the text field labeled Name at the top-left corner of the Object Properties box. Delete the name object0 and type "CashObject" in its place.

The next step is to assign a sprite to this object. This will allow us to see the object when it is placed inside a game room. To do this, move your cursor to the textbox that says "no sprite" and left-click on it. You will see a drop-down list of possible sprites that you could choose from, as shown in Figure 2.11. Choose the sprite named Cash.

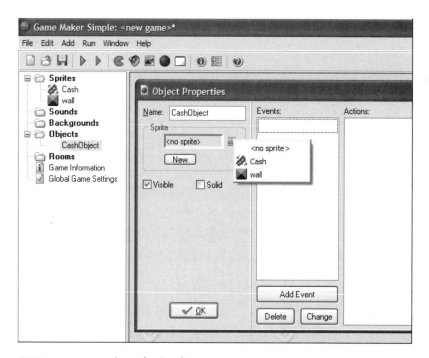

FIGURE 2.11   Sprite Selection list.

After assigning the object with a sprite, let's close the object by clicking on the OK button at the bottom of the Object Properties window.

Just as we created the CashObject, let's create one more object and rename it BrickObject. In the Object Properties sheet, let's assign the Wall sprite to this object and then click the OK button to close the Object properties dialog box.

We now have two sprites and two objects in our resource tree.

CREATING GAME ROOMS

We are now ready to create a game room and place the two objects that we have created into it. To create a new room, click on the Create New Room icon (Figure 2.12) on the Main Toolbar.

FIGURE 2.12   Create New Room icon.

You should see a Room Properties dialog box appear in the Workspace area, as shown in Figure 2.13. You can maximize the Room Properties dialog box by clicking on the maximize button on the upper-righthand side corner of the dialog box.

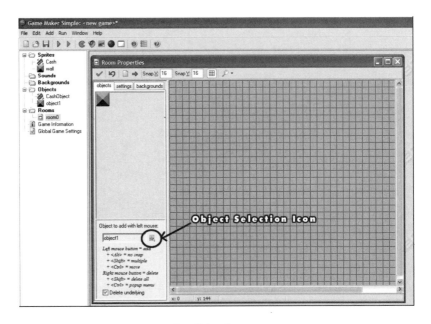

FIGURE 2.13   Room Properties dialog box.

We are now ready to place our objects in our game room. The game room becomes alive when it is populated with objects. The game room is currently an empty grid of squares, and as you move your mouse around the grid, you should see the coordinates labeled X and Y traversed shown on the status line at the bottom of the dialog box. The coordinates show you the location of objects contained in the game room.

To add objects to the game room, click on the Object Selection icon located inside the Object Properties dialog box shown in Figure 2.13. You should see a list of possible choices appear in a drop-down menu, as shown in Figure 2.14.

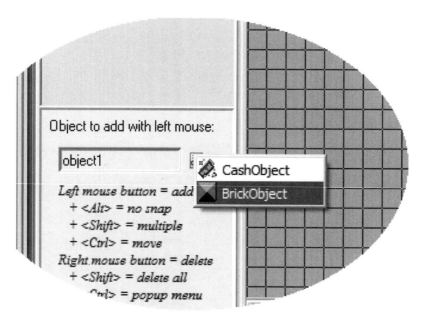

FIGURE 2.14   Object Selection drop-down menu.

Choose the BrickObject selection. If you move over to the grid area and left-click anywhere, you should see an instance of the BrickObject placed at that spot. Now let's place a set of brick objects to form a rectangle, as shown in Figure 2.15. If a brick object has been placed in the wrong spot, you can use the right mouse button to remove the object.

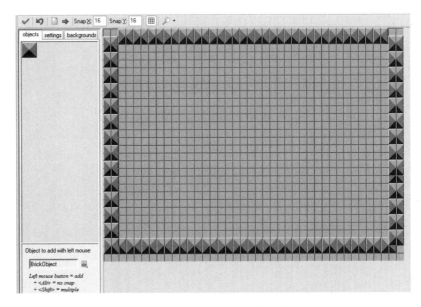

FIGURE 2.15   Multiple `BrickObjects` placed in the new room.

You can hold the Shift key down and then click and drag your left mouse button to place multiple instances of the object wherever you choose.

Now, using the same procedure we used to place several instances of the `BrickObject`, let's select the `CashObject` and place a few instances of it inside the rectangle formed by the `BrickObjects`. You need to first choose the `CashObject` from the list of choices in the drop-down menu that show up when you click on the Object Selection icon (Figures 2.13 and 2.14). Left-click on a few spots inside the rectangular grid formed by the `BrickObjects`. Let's place three `CashObjects` at approximate locations, as shown in Figure 2.16.

Now let's run the game by pressing the Run Game icon—the green arrow pointing to your right on the Main Toolbar. You should see your screen briefly change to the Game Loading screen, followed by the game you created.

You should be able to see all the bricks and the cash objects. You will immediately note that there is no real game to play here. All the objects are stationary, and there is nothing you can do except press the Escape key to quit the game.

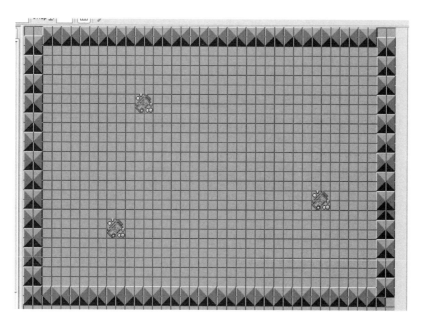

FIGURE 2.16   CashObjects placed inside the game room.

The reason behind this uneventful behavior from the stationary objects is that the stationary objects do not have any intelligence. All we did was create the object and assign it a sprite so that we could view it in our game. We did not instruct our objects on how they should interact with their environment or other internal events. This brings us to a brief discussion about objects and their lifecycle and how internal events, external events, and actions define their behavior.

OBJECT LIFECYCLE

Just like living objects in the real world, game objects go through lifecycles. They are born, they live a finite lifetime, and then they die. During their lifetimes, all objects are informed of different kinds of events that occur. For example, we human beings may hear on the radio that a new restaurant is opening in our neighborhood. This is one kind of event that we can become aware of. Obviously, there are several thousands of such events that we can process and respond to during our lifetime. We have a very complex event-response system.

Game Objects, on the other hand, have a simple lifecycle system. They respond only to a few events by executing certain limited actions. Game Objects receive two important events during their lifetimes. The first event is the Create event and the other is the Destroy event. An object receives the Create event when it is born and it receives the Destroy event just before it dies. In the case of the CashObjects, we want all of them to start moving as soon as they are born. Therefore, we have to program our CashObject to respond to a Create event by moving in a specific direction. Let's now see how to make our CashObjects respond to events.

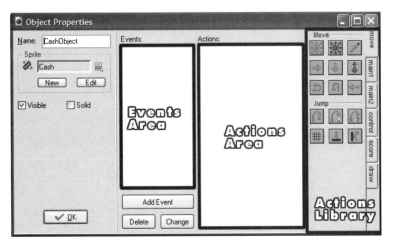

FIGURE 2.17   Different areas of the Object Properties box.

In the Resource Explorer window, double-click on the CashObject selection. This will open up the CashObjects' properties dialog box, as shown in Figure 2.17. You may notice an empty Events Area under a text field called Events as well as another empty Actions Area under a text field labeled Actions. Initially, the CashObject does not respond to any event and does not do anything. That explains why we saw static objects when we ran our first version of the game.

ADDING EVENTS

To make our game interesting, we need objects that will respond to various events by performing different actions. To make the CashObject move as soon as it is created, we are going to program it to respond to the Create event. Although many beginners feel nervous when they hear the term *programming*, we can assure you that there is nothing to fear. Programming the CashObject simply means we tell the CashObject how to respond to different events. We will provide instructions to the CashObject on when and how it should perform certain tasks. Let's start with making the CashObject move.

Click on the Add Event button found under the Events Area. This should open up the Event Selector dialog box, as shown in Figure 2.18.

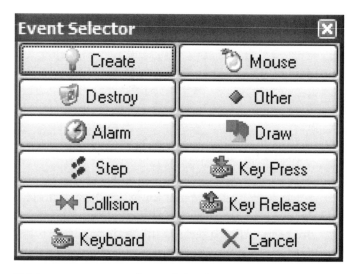

FIGURE 2.18   Event Selector dialog box.

The Event Selector box gives you a complete list of all events a Game Object can respond to. We are interested in the Create event, so let's click on the Create event (Figure 2.19).

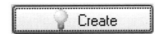

FIGURE 2.19 Create Event selector.

Once the Create event is clicked, you should see it added to the Events Area.

ADDING ACTIONS

Now that we have the Create event added to the events area, we can define what actions the objects will perform when this event occurs. Several kinds of actions are available in the Actions Library area shown in Figure 2.17. They are categorized into functional areas. You can click on the different tabs in the Action Library Area and get an overview of the kinds of actions that an object can perform. Placing your mouse over each of the actions displays a tool-tip textbox that describes what the action does.

To make an object move, we need to select the first action (Figure 2.20) found under the Move tab. Click and drag this action button from the Actions Library area onto the Actions Area. Once this is done, your screen should look like the one shown in Figure 2.21.

At this point, you have the Create event that triggers the Move action. To complete the Move action, we need to define the direction and speed in which the object should move. Let's make the object move at a speed of four units toward the lower-right corner. With these settings, the Action Properties box should look like Figure 2.22.

FIGURE 2.20 Action to make an object start moving.

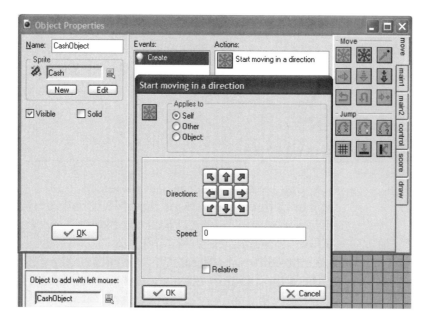

FIGURE 2.21 `Create` Event and Action response.

Click the OK button on the Action Property box shown in Figure 2.22. Next click on the Run Game icon in the Main Toolbar.

The `CashObjects` now move. They all disappear after a few seconds, and there is nothing wrong with what they are doing for they have now been programmed to move as soon as they are born. Now let's confine the `CashObjects` to stay within the room we have created with the `BrickObjects`. To do this, we need to make the `CashObject` bounce when it collides against a `BrickObject`.

FIGURE 2.22 Move Action property box.

ADDING A COLLISION EVENT

Let's go to the Properties Sheet for the CashObject by double-clicking on the CashObject in the Resource Explorer area. Click on the Add Event button to display the Event Selector dialog box, as shown in Figure 2.18. We are now interested in executing an action when a Collision event occurs. To do this, choose the Collision Event selection from the Event Selector dialog box, as shown in Figure 2.23.

As soon as you click on the Collision Event selector, you will be prompted with a list of possible objects that you could collide against, as shown in Figure 2.24.

Since we are providing instructions for what the CashObject should do when it collides against the BrickObject, we need to choose the BrickObject from the list shown in Figure 2.24.

FIGURE 2.23 `Collision` event.

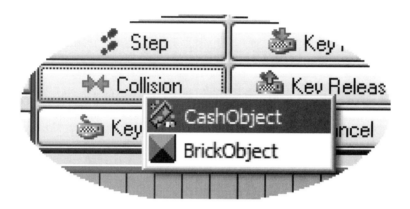

FIGURE 2.24 `Collision` Object selection list.

Once that is selected, your `CashObject`'s property sheet should have two events, as shown in Figure 2.25—the `Create` event and the `Collision` Event. Take a moment to notice that you could select either event by clicking on the appropriate event in the events area. Selecting an event highlights the event in blue. Any actions dragged from the library area to the actions area are applied to the highlighted event in the event area.

Now let's add some actions to the `Collision` event. Make sure the `Collision` event of the `CashObject` is highlighted, as shown in Figure 2.25. We are now ready to provide instructions to the `CashObject` on what it should do when it collides with the `BrickObject`.

One instruction we can give the `CashObject` is to have it bounce off the wall. This can be done using the using the Bounce Against Objects action (Figure 2.26) found under the Move tab of the Library area. Click and drag the `Bounce` Action from the library area onto the Actions area.

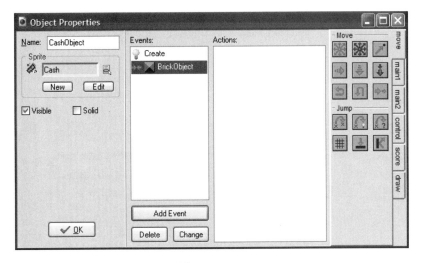

FIGURE 2.25   CashObject with two events.

FIGURE 2.26   Bounce action.

You will be presented with another dialog box (Figure 2.27) that can be used to customize the Bounce action. The default setting needs to be changed to make sure the CashObject bounces against all objects. Make the changes highlighted in Figure 2.27. Click OK to close the Bounce Action dialog box. Now it is time to test your game.

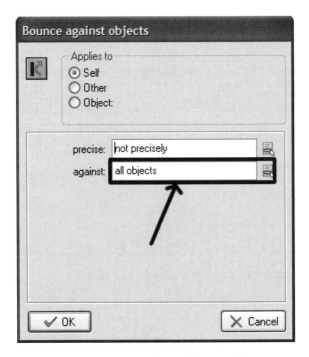

FIGURE 2.27   Bounce Against Objects setting.

Let's run the game. You should see some action now. The CashObjects should be happily bouncing around. Now comes the exciting part. We need to reward the player. Close the game so that we can proceed to the next step of adding a score count to the game.

ADDING SCORE

Now that we have the CashObjects moving around, let's award five points for each time the player clicks on one of them. To do this, we need the CashObject to be able to respond to another event. This event would be the Mouse-Click event. When this event occurs, we need to find a library action that we could use to increase our score by five points. (Of course, you can be as generous as you want to with your points in order to make your game players excited and happy.)

Let's go back and make the `CashObject` the active object by double-clicking on it in the Resource Explorer. Let's add the `Mouse-Click` event by first clicking on the Add Event button in the `CashObjects` Property dialog box. You will see the Event Selector dialog box (Figure 2.18) appear. Click on the Mouse Event button to reveal a list of options, as shown in Figure 2.28. Choose the Left Button option. This will be our button of choice that will be used to accumulate points.

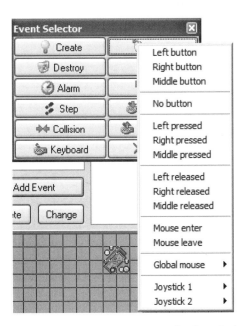

FIGURE 2.28   Mouse Event Selection List box.

Now we are ready to use the Set Score Library action found under the Score tab of the Actions Library. Activate the Score tab by clicking on it. Click and drag the Set Score action from the library area to the Actions Area, as shown in Figure 2.29. You will be prompted with the Set Score dialog box.

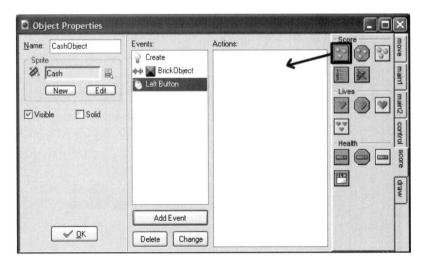

FIGURE 2.29 Set Score action.

The Set Score dialog box is the place to input the score that has to be added. Enter an input value of five as shown in Figure 2.30. Also, make sure you check the Relative box located underneath the New Score Input box. This box will make changes to your score relative to what it was earlier.

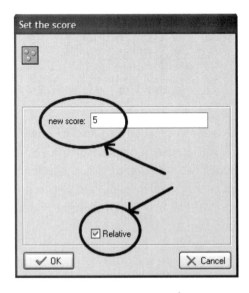

FIGURE 2.30 Set Score Action

Thus, the player's score will increase by five points only if the Relative button has been unchecked.

PLAYING THE GAME

Now it is time to save the file. Click on the File menu and then select the Save option. Save your game as ClickOn-CashV1 in a directory of your choice.

Congratulations! You have created your first game. Now it is time to play and enjoy your first game. Click on the flying cash and see what happens to your score.

SUMMARY

In this chapter, we learned basic concepts of objects, events, and actions. We learned about the Game Maker User Interface, created objects, and placed them in game rooms. We discussed the lifecycle of objects and understood the significance of the Create and Destroy events. We also made objects perform a sequence of actions in response to different events, looked at Collision events, and used actions in the Score tab to award points to the user. In addition, we also created our first game, ClickOnCash, that awards you points when you click on the cash objects that fly inside the room.

Projects

Here are additional things to try: 1) Add another object—maybe diamonds—that are also found inside the room. Let them move at double the speed of the cash object. When the user clicks on these diamonds, let the user be awarded twice the points as that of the cash object. 2) Now, try adding another object—maybe fire—that is found inside the room. Clicking on these objects takes away points from the user.

These take the role of enemy objects found in a traditional game that takes away part of the score.

If you want to make the game more difficult, place a few more fire objects in the room, which makes it harder to accumulate points. You may even find your score going negative, if there are too many of these objects. We'll learn how to exit the game before the score becomes a negative value in subsequent chapters.

CHAPTER 3

Using the Image and Sprite Editor

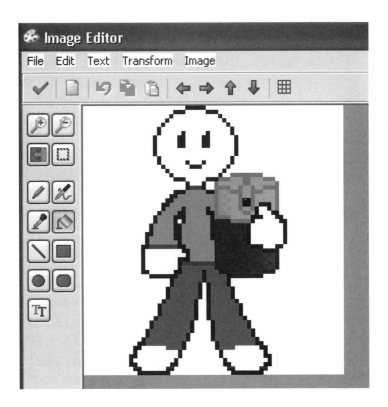

In this chapter:

- ▪ Creating a New Background
- ▪ The Drawing Tools
- ▪ The Text Tool
- ▪ Using Gradients
- ▪ The Transformation Tools

Before we embark on creating captivating games, we need to be able to create custom sprites that suit our requirements. Game Maker comes with a set of self-contained image editing tools that could be used for creating all kinds of colorful animated sprites and backgrounds. The Image Editor and Sprite Editor that come with Game Maker are used to create custom images and sprites. The Image Editor contains a set of drawing tools and features like those found in many image editing applications. It is nicely integrated into the Game Maker application, making it easy to use. The Sprite Editor provides functionality to animate, scale, rotate, colorize, and provide special effects that make the sprite look dynamic and alive. The Sprite Editor supports the importing of different kinds of image files such as jpeg, bmp, gif, and many more.

In this chapter, we will introduce you to the image editing features available and create the backgrounds and sprites that will be used in the games we will build in subsequent chapters. The game Swat the Bugs described in Chapter 7 requires several backgrounds and sprites. As examples, we will create one background and one animated sprite that will provide you with sufficient insight to create your own game assets.

CREATING A NEW BACKGROUND

Let's start a new game with Game Maker. Note the empty resource tree on the left. This indicates that you are in a new game. Now, let's create a new background by clicking on the Add a Background icon on the toolbar, as shown in Figure 3.1. Alternatively, a new background can be added by right-clicking on the Backgrounds label in the Resource Explorer and then choosing the Add Background option from the pop-up menu.

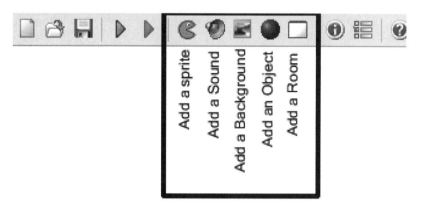

FIGURE 3.1   Add Assets icons.

The Background Properties dialog box shown in Figure 3.2 should be visible on the screen. It is a good practice to change the Name field to reflect the name of the asset. Since we are creating a background for the Swat the Bug game, let's rename the background "grass." Now we are ready to create the background. Click on the Edit Background button on the Background Properties dialog box and the Image Editor (Figure 3.3) will appear.

The Image Editor consists of four pieces. The Drawing Tools on the left consist of a set of basic drawing tools that could be used for creating sprites and backgrounds. The Color Chooser on the right allows you to choose two colors and keep them handy for use with the different tools. These two colors are shown at the top of the Color Browser window and are labeled Left and Right. Based on the chosen drawing tool, the color labeled Left is applied by left-clicking and the color labeled Right is applied by right-clicking. The colors beneath the Left and Right labels in the Color Chooser window can be changed by clicking on either square beneath them. A pop-up Color Browser window should be visible when you left-click on the square. Choosing a color and then clicking on the OK button will make the newly selected color active.

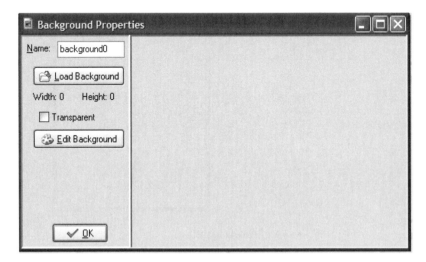

FIGURE 3.2   Background Properties dialog box.

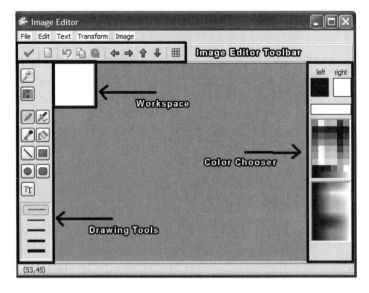

FIGURE 3.3   Image Editor.

The Image Editor Toolbar consists of icons that can be used to move images in different directions. One way of creating animated sprites is to create a base image and then create a set of sequential images using that base image by moving the image inside its canvas in different directions. The area marked Workspace is the active region where the drawing tools can be used to create backgrounds and sprites. You may have noticed that the Workspace is small in Figure 3.3. This is too small for creating an elaborate background. The size might be right if we were planning to use the tiling concept, where we create a small image that can be duplicated several times and placed as tiles to create a 2D background scene. If the canvas size of the background in the Image Editor is small, it can be resized by going to the Transform > Resize Canvas menu item.

For our first exercise, let's embark on creating a grassy image that could be used in our game. Let's also plan on creating the small image that can be aggregated and tiled together to create a larger background. The size of images on the computer is measured in pixels. A *pixel* is a single dot displayed on the screen. There are approximately 100 to 200 pixels per inch on the computer screen. The following paragraph describes why we define the size of the image we intend to create to be 64 pixels wide.

If we create an image that is 64 pixels wide and 64 pixels high and our game requires a background of 640 pixels by 480 pixels, then we would need to fill up the background with the appropriate number of images horizontally and vertically. To be precise, we would need ten columns of images horizontally to cover the width of 640 pixels (64 pixels × 10 columns = 640 pixels). We would need several rows of images to cover the vertical height. Seven and a half rows would be required to cover 480 pixels. Thus, to cover an area of 640 × 480 pixels we would need 75 images (10 × 7.5) tiled in rows and columns. If the image were created so that the boundaries match when they are tiled, the user would not be able to guess the size of the images used to create the background.

Let's first check to see if the canvas size is 64 × 64 pixels. Click on the Transform > Resize Canvas menu item. A Resize pop-up menu will appear. Modify the width and height to 64 pixels and then close the Resize dialog box.

You may have noticed that the Workspace is tiny. An area of 64 × 64 pixels is a tiny amount of space and it may seem impossible to draw anything on it. The Zoom tool placed at the top-left corner of the Drawing Toolbar alleviates this problem. Clicking on the Plus button zooms into the image and clicking on the Minus button zooms out. If there is no more room to zoom out, the Minus button is not displayed. Let's use the Zoom tool to magnify our view of the image and then start creating the grassy texture.

THE DRAWING TOOLS

Before we start creating images we can use in our game, it is a good idea to examine the drawing tools that we have at our disposal. Although it is possible to import images from other graphic design software, it is very convenient to create images quickly using the drawing tools shown in Figure 3.4.

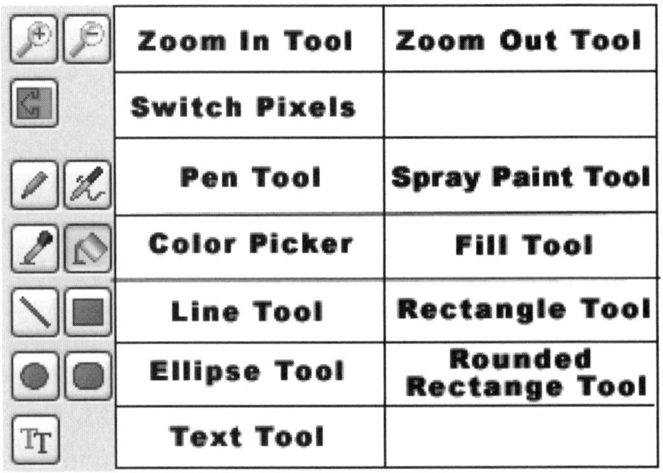

	Zoom In Tool	Zoom Out Tool
	Switch Pixels	
	Pen Tool	Spray Paint Tool
	Color Picker	Fill Tool
	Line Tool	Rectangle Tool
	Ellipse Tool	Rounded Rectange Tool
	Text Tool	

FIGURE 3.4   Drawing tools.

We are familiar with the two tools in the first row that allows us to zoom in and zoom out. Let's investigate the Pen tool. Left-clicking on any of the tools in the Drawing Tools box activates the selected tool. Depending on the selected tool, it may have several options. For example, if you selected the Pen tool, you should see the options displayed in Figure 3.5.

FIGURE 3.5   Pen tools options.

The Pen tool options are the same as the brush size for a brush tool in other software packages. Select the line size by clicking on the segment size of your choice. Spend a minute trying to draw lines of different colors and sizes in the Workspace using the pen tool. After choosing the Pen tool, left-clicking and dragging it in the Workspace area creates a line. Right-clicking and dragging in the Workspace creates a line with the color attached to the right-mouse button in the Color Chooser box. At this point, you should be able to quickly draw lines and shapes using the left- and right-mouse buttons. Depending on the color assigned to these buttons, you should see appropriate graphics on the Workspace.

To create the texture of grass, let's first select a tint of green and assign it to the Left label of the Color Chooser box. Doing this creates a shortcut for using the selected green color. Left-clicking and dragging in the Workspace with the pen tool selected creates green lines. To simulate a natural grassy area, it may be best to fill the area with the green color. We can do this by switching to the Fill Tool icon by left-clicking on the icon in the Drawing Tools section shown in Figure 3.4. Once the Fill Tool is selected, the options in the Drawing Tools section disappear since there are no valid options. The fill tool allows us to pour paint into the Workspace. Now it is time to flood the Workspace with green by left-clicking on it.

We now have a green image that will be part of our grassy area. To make this look realistic, let's now create some yellow flowering dandelions. To do this we are going to use the Spray Paint tool and assign a shade of yellow to the right mouse button. On completion of this step, your background image should look like that shown in Figure 3.6. It is now time to close and save changes in the Image Editor by clicking on the Check Mark in the Image Editor toolbar.

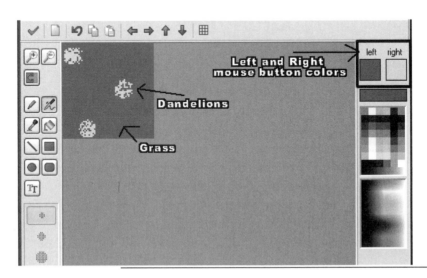

FIGURE 3.6   Background image.

The Line tool, Rectangle tool, Ellipse tool, and Rounded Rectangle tool all work in a similar fashion. They have different options such as fill and borders that you could experiment and become familiar with. You could create a new background and use it as a little playpen to try these tools out. After that you could either delete this background or just leave it dormant in your game for now. You can delete any unwanted entity in Game Maker by right-clicking on it in the Resource Explorer and then choosing the delete option in the pop-up menu, as shown in Figure 3.7.

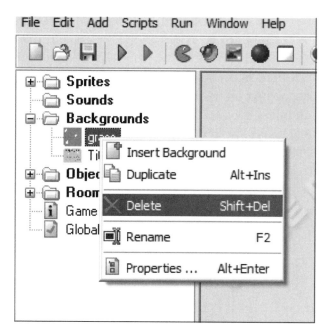

FIGURE 3.7   Deleting entities.

THE TEXT TOOL

The Text tool is useful for creating readable text. It is activated by left-clicking on the Text tool icon shown back in Figure 3.4. The font's size and style can be changed by choosing the

Text > Font menu option. Placing text in the Workspace is as simple as placing your cursor at the desired position with a left- or right-mouse button click and then typing in the text.

Let's use the Text tool to create the background for the title screen of our game. Create a new background as we did in the earlier section (click on the Add a Background icon found in the Main Toolbar) when we created the grassy background. You should see the Background Properties dialog box. Let's rename the background "TitleScreen." Click on the Edit button to go to the Image Editor once again. Since we are creating a title screen, we would like the workspace to be bigger than the default 64×64 pixels. Click on Transform > Resize Canvas to go to the Resize Options dialog box shown in Figure 3.8. We would like the background image size to be 640×480 pixels. Modify this in the Resize Options dialog box by unchecking the Keep Aspect Ratio check box and then by entering the values of 640 pixels for Width and 480 pixels for Height. The completed dialog box is shown in Figure 3.8. Click OK and you will see the Workspace enlarge. You may need to resize the Image Editor window to see the complete workspace.

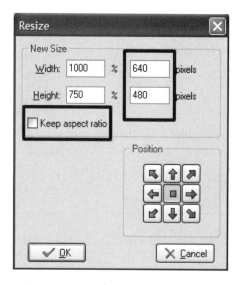

FIGURE 3.8   Resize Options.

Using Gradients

To make the background more attractive, you could use the gradient options found in the Image Menu. Clicking on Image > Gradient Fill opens up the Gradient Fill dialog box, as shown in Figure 3.9.

FIGURE 3.9   Gradient Options. (See Color version on companion CD-ROM)

You can choose the first color and the second color by clicking on the default color boxes displayed to the right of these labels. You could also choose the type of gradient by left-clicking on one of the six sample gradient boxes. Several coloring options are in the Image Menu for customizing the gradients. Try the different options out and familiarize yourself with them. Clicking the OK button applies the gradient to the background.

Now that we have a background color, left-click on the Text tool found in the Drawing Tools area. Before we click on the Workspace to type in any information, let's change the text font and size using the Text > Font menu item. You can experiment with different fonts and sizes to choose an appropriate combination. In this example, we have chosen Times New Roman with a font size of 72. You can add all kinds of text and images to make this page attractive. In later chapters we will add intelligent objects that need to be clicked on to start the game and other objects that play music. Your finished title screen may look like the one shown in Figure 3.10. Save and close your changes when you have completed creating your title screen.

FIGURE 3.10   Finished background. Courtesy of Ramya Swamy. Reprinted with permission.

THE TRANSFORM TOOLS

The transform tools provided in the Image Editor and the Sprite Editor can be used for rotating, mirroring, and scaling images. Let's investigate the use of the transform tools found in the Sprite Editor.

    In our game we need a spray can that can be pointed in four directions. To do this let's first create a new sprite by clicking on the Add a Sprite icon in the Main Toolbar. Let's rename it player_left in the Sprite Properties dialog box. Now click on the Edit Sprite button to draw our spray can. You should be transported to the Sprite Editor, as shown in Figure 3.11. In the Sprite Editor window, you will see an image of an empty sprite labeled Image 0. This image needs to be edited to create the image of the spray can. Double-clicking on the square image just above the label Image 0 should take you back to the Image Editor.

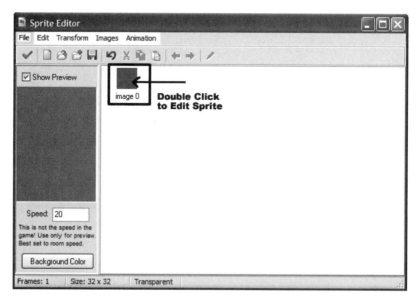

FIGURE 3.11   Sprite Editor.

In this Image Editor, let's first set the canvas size to 96 × 96 pixels. Once that is done, you can use all the drawing tools at your disposal and create a picture of a player carrying a bug repellant canister as shown in Figure 3.12.

After you have created the picture, click on the Check Mark on the Image Editor to save and close the changes. You should be transported back to the Sprite Editor. Enabling the Preview Check Box in the Sprite Editor will show you what the sprite looks like when it is incorporated into a game. Save your changes and close the Sprite Editor by clicking on the green Check Mark on the Sprite Editor tool bar. You can also close the Sprite Properties dialog box by clicking on the OK button.

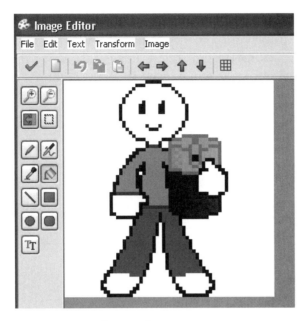

FIGURE 3.12   Player Sprite. Images courtesy of Ramya Swamy. Reprinted with permission.

Now that we have one player sprite created, we can transform the geometry using the transform tools to create three more player sprites that will emit bug-spray in the other three directions. Let's duplicate the sprite we created by right-clicking on the `player_left` sprite and choosing the Duplicate option from the pop-up menu, as shown in Figure 3.13.

Game Maker has created one more sprite for you with an automatically assigned name. Let's rename this sprite `player_right` and then go to the Sprite Editor by clicking on the Edit button. In the Sprite Editor, let's horizontally mirror the sprite by using the Transform > Mirror Horizontal button. Save the changes and close the Sprite Editor.

ON THE CD

For the player up and down sprites, let's load the files provided to you on the CD-ROM. Let's start working on the `player_down` sprite. Right-click on the Sprites folder in the Resource Explorer and choose Add Sprite from the drop-down menu. This takes you to the Sprites Properties Editor. In the Sprites Properties Editor, let's type "player_down" in

ON THE CD

the text box labeled Name. Click on the Load Image button and select the file Resources\Sprites\player_down.bmp from the CD-ROM, as shown in Figure 3.14. That completes the process of creating the player_down sprite. You can now repeat this process to create the player_up sprite.

FIGURE 3.13 Duplicate option.

FIGURE 3.14 Duplicate Option.

This procedure can be summarized as follows:

- Duplicate an existing player sprite.
- Go to the Sprite Editor and rotate and transform the sprite as necessary.
- Save and close changes.

At the end of this process, you should have four sprites, as shown in Figure 3.15.

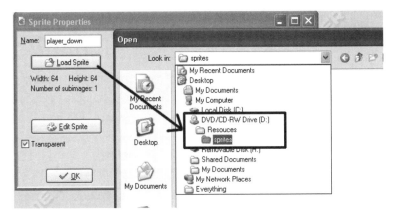

FIGURE 3.15   Completed sprites.

We now have completed creating sprites and backgrounds that will be used to create the Swat the Bug game, including the title screen, the player, and the background images. We are ready to build objects, attach behaviors, place them in game rooms, and then play the game.

Now it is time to save the game for use in future chapters. Save this file as Chapter 3 in your local directory.

SUMMARY

In this chapter, we looked at the graphics tools that come embedded with Game Maker. Although there are several other tools that could be used, a lot of the work can be done easily using just the Sprite Editor and the Image Editor. As we learned, backgrounds for games can be created to fit the size of the game room using a set of Drawing tools provided with the Image Editor. Gradients, text, and paint tools can be used to create nice sprites. The Image Editor also has several features that could be used to create animated sprites. Look through these and try out the features provided in the Transform and Image sub-menus.

Projects

If you already have a game idea you would like to implement, you should be in a position to start building the sprites for that game. 1) You can use the external editor and import the images, if you think that would work better for you. You could also experiment with the editor and create additional title screens and background images. 2) Remember that you can use the Image Editor's Transform tools to flip images along horizontal and vertical axes to create images of objects moving in different directions. You can also shrink and enlarge images and create animated sprites.

CHAPTER 4

Introduction to Object Technology

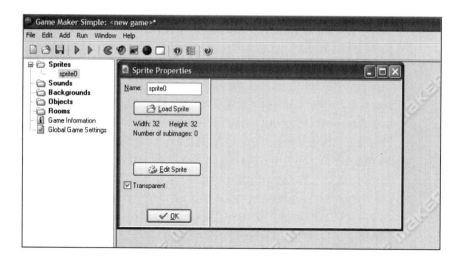

In this chapter:

- What is Object Technology?
- Defining Object Behaviors
- Describing Object Properties
- Visualizing Object Hierarchy
- Generalization Concepts
- Behavior Encapsulation
- Polymorphism

We will now look at software development techniques that have evolved into a paradigm that perfectly fits the Game Design industry. Experts are talking about object-oriented programming methodology as the right way to develop software. In this methodology, one can view the system as a set of objects that work together to produce a well-defined output. Games can be visualized in terms of interacting objects. *Pacman*, for instance, uses the Pacman object that has the appearance of a smiley face. The Pacman object also has different behaviors that define its characteristics. For example, if the player presses the left arrow key, Pacman moves to the left at a defined speed. If the Pacman collides against a bonus object, the user gets bonus points added to his score. If the Pacman collides against a monster object, Pacman looses one life. If Pacman looses three lives, the user looses the game.

In *Pacman*, we create an object with a set of behaviors that defines its characteristics. Some of the behaviors of the Pacman object are listed below:

- If the user presses the left arrow, move left.
- If the user presses the right arrow, move right.
- If the user presses the up arrow, move up.
- If the user presses the down arrow, move down.
- If there is a collision with a dot object, add five points to the users score.

- If there is a collision with a monster object, reduce the health by one. If health is less than zero, end the game.
- If there is a collision with the wall, set the speed to zero (stop the Pacman).

These behaviors can be thought of as a set of actions that trigger a set of reactions. The action that an object responds to and the reaction it exhibits can be different for any type of object. In *Pacman*, if the user presses the up arrow key, the Pacman object moves up. On the other hand, the wall object ignores all actions related to the keyboard. The wall object does not care if the user presses the up arrow or the down arrow. It ignores all events.

WHAT IS OBJECT TECHNOLOGY?

As we mentioned in Chapter 2, we view the world as a set of independent objects that interact with each other. If you look at the world around you, you will find millions of objects and millions of different kinds of interactions between objects. We can view computer games as the interaction of a set of independent objects. Game Maker provides a way to create the objects, give them a specific appearance, and then provide them with a set of predefined behaviors.

DEFINING OBJECT BEHAVIORS

For objects to interact with one other, they need to be able to perform specific actions. These actions are called *behaviors* in object technology. For example, the actions that a mouse can perform (i.e., its behaviors) include the ability to see, run, walk, bite, sleep, turn, and more. The mouse is a self-contained object with well-defined behaviors. If you take a moment and look at the objects around you, you will find that all object have well-defined behaviors.

If you look at a television, for example, you will see that the actions that the television can perform include the following: display a picture, play a sound track, change channels, turn on and off, and more. Some of these actions are performed by interaction with the remote control, which is another object.

What about a chair? What are its behaviors? A chair basically sits in one place. If it has a cushion, the cushion gets compressed when someone sits on it. That is its main behavior. If too many people sit on it, it may break. That could be another behavior. Start to think about various objects and the different behaviors they might encompass.

With this introduction to objects and behaviors, we should now be able to easily isolate objects and identify their behaviors when they interact with other objects. This is a key concept to understand in the creation of a computer game.

DESCRIBING OBJECT PROPERTIES

Apart from behaviors, objects have properties that define them. Behaviors are usually described using verbs that depict a particular action an object can perform. Properties, on the other hand, describe the characteristics of an object. An object's properties also typically describe what it looks like. A mouse object may have the following properties (Table 4.1):

TABLE 4.1

Object Property	Property Value
Color	Gray
Weight	12 ounces
Tail Length	3 inches
Fur Coat Type	Smooth

VISUALIZING OBJECT HIERARCHY

Think again of the television. Once we create an object that represents a television, we do not need to recreate things from scratch in order to create a brand new television. All televisions have a common set of behaviors. Although different brands may have different additional features, they all contain the following *base features*.

■ On-off switch
■ Volume control
■ Channel switch
■ Brightness control

An object that contains all of the basic features necessary to define a particular object is called the *parent object* or the *base object*. In our example of the television, the base television object contains four of the above-mentioned features.

If Sony made a new television that had built-in games and if General Electric made one that had Internet connectivity, we would have two special television objects. These two objects inherit features from the base television object, but they contain their own additional features. These two new objects would be called the *subclasses* of the parent object.

In summary, object technology permits inheritance of features from a parent object, making it unnecessary to reinvent the wheel and create everything from scratch. This makes game design easy and fun to do.

GENERALIZATION CONCEPTS

Now that we have a good understanding of objects, their behaviors, and their properties, we can start creating objects that could be used in games. Before objects are created for a game, it is beneficial to design the objects and investigate the possibility of finding other objects with similar properties.

Whenever you are designing objects for any game, you need to first extract all of the common attributes of objects and put them into a base object. This procedure of extracting common features is called *generalization.*

If certain objects have certain special features, they need to be defined in new subclasses that *inherit* behaviors from their parent object.

For example, let's say that in a game you have a mouse object and a rabbit object and that the user is required to control and move each of these objects using the cursor keys. It may be a good idea to extract this common feature and implement it in a parent object named animal. The mouse and the rabbit could then inherit the features from the animal object, such as being four legged and furry. This would not only save you time, but it would make your game concise and easy to maintain.

BEHAVIOR ENCAPSULATION

In object-oriented languages such as Java and C++, it is possible to *encapsulate* data and services such that the complexity of the object is not visible to users of the object. Game Maker objects are independent encapsulated objects that have specific properties and behaviors. In the game room, these objects interact with other objects and behave just like objects we see every day in the real world. For example, the mouse object has encapsulated behaviors that make it move away from an eagle object, and a cup has encapsulated behaviors that make it able to hold liquids.

POLYMORPHISM

Polymorphism is the ability of two or more objects to perform different actions in response to the same event. Objects are polymorphic. For example, if a mouse object receives a keyboard event, it may start walking in one direction. On the other hand, if an eagle object receives the same keyboard event, it may start flying in another direction. Polymorphism is the ability of different objects to invoke different behaviors for the same event. For example, if you create a boat object, a car object, and a plane object, you can send them a "move" command. The boat will move on water after turning on onboard motors, the car will move after turning on its engine, and the plane will move after turning on its jet engines.

With this firm understanding of object technology, it's time to design games using object technology.

SUMMARY

In this chapter, we looked at the core components of Object technology. We compared the real world with the objects in a game, and described the properties and behaviors of objects. We also looked at object hierarchy and stressed the importance of extracting the common behaviors into a parent object, and learned that encapsulation is the process of embedding properties and behaviors into an object. And finally, we learned that Polymorphism is the property of objects to behave differently in response to the same external event.

Projects

As an exercise, think of all the game objects that would be required in a game of your choice. Explore the objects in detail and list out the events they will respond to, and enumerate the actions that will be executed during each event.

Keyboard Control for Objects

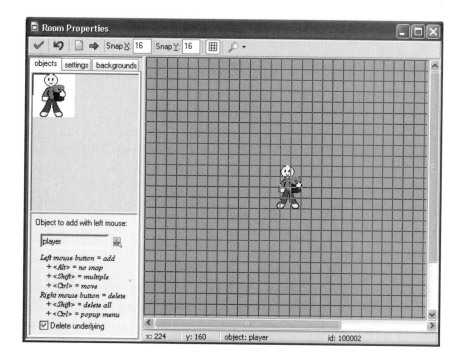

In this chapter:

- Sprites and Objects
- The Art of Building the Game Room
- Creating the Game
- Adding a Room
- Modifying the Object's Appearance

In this chapter we are going to be building a game in which we have to exterminate bugs using an aerosol repellant. We will be incrementally adding features starting from the simplest requirements and progressing to more difficult ones later. We have already created sprites for the player object running around with a repellant in Chapter 3. Let's create a room where we can move the player around using our keyboard controls. The up, down, left, and right arrow keys will move the player in the appropriate direction.

To begin, you could either open up the file you saved at the end of Chapter 3 or load the Game Maker file Chapter5/ Example5.1.gm6 from the CD-ROM. It has a couple of sprites and backgrounds that we created earlier.

ON THE CD

SPRITES AND OBJECTS

Recall that sprites are the little pictures that are created with the Sprite Editor. They could also be created by using an external image editor and then imported into Game Maker. Sprites are just like the user interface for Game Maker objects. If you want objects to be visible in a game, you need to define them using sprites. Sprites provide a visual clue as to how the object looks. They do not have any built-in *actions*. They cannot move, play music, or vanish. In other words, sprites do not have actions, for they are simply a visual form. Comparing the picture of a dog (a sprite) with a real dog (an object) will show the differences between a sprite and an object. A sprite cannot bark or move, but is visible. A dog can bark, can move, and is visible. An object without a sprite becomes invisible. An object is an entity that is encapsulated with behaviors and properties that could be used in a game. A game object could be thought of as an intelligent sprite. Objects have behaviors that sprites are devoid of. A dog object, for example, can run, bark, and wag its tail. A car object can go forward, backward, and turn. A computer object can play music, display images on its screen, and run many applications.

THE ART OF BUILDING A GAME ROOM

Games take place in game rooms. The game room is where the game objects interact with one other and with the game player. In Game Maker, the game room is a 2D area—the size of which can be customized. The size of the game room is defined in pixels, and the default values for the game room are 640 pixels in width and 480 pixels in height.

Game objects positioned inside the room have their positions defined by a pair of X and Y coordinates. X is the distance from the left margin of the room and Y defines the distance from the top of the room, as shown in Figure 5.1

We need to take note of a couple of things with respect to the game room. The X coordinate increases in value toward the right. The Y coordinate increases in value toward the bottom of the screen. Thus, on an object that moves up the screen, we can understand why its Y coordinate value decreases. Game objects can also travel in different directions in the game room. These directions are specified as angles with respect to the horizontal. Thus, if we have an object moving at a speed of ten pixels per second at an angle of 180 degrees, we know it is moving toward the negative X direction. An angle of 90 degrees points up and an angle of 270 degrees points down.

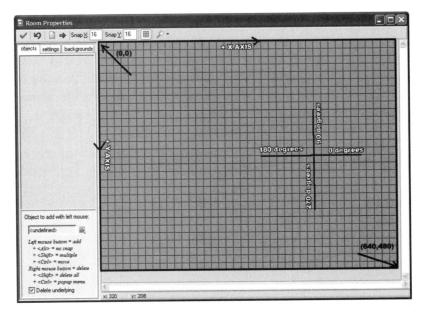

FIGURE 5.1 Game room geometry.

Understanding the game room geometry is important. When objects are dynamically assigned various positions, we can see how movement and speed differ.

The following table shows the valid entries for the direction of movement of an object when different cursor keys are pressed. For example, when the up arrow key is pressed, the objects moves 0 units in the X direction and −5 units in the Y direction (Table 5.1).

TABLE 5.1

Cursor Key	X Value	Y Value
Up Arrow	0	−5
Down Arrow	0	5
Left Arrow	−5	0
Right Arrow	5	0

CREATING THE GAME

Now that we have an understanding of sprites, objects, game rooms, and backgrounds, let's apply them to create a game.

If you haven't yet loaded up the game, load the game provided on the CD-ROM from the directory Chapter5\Example5.1.gm6. You should see a couple of sprites and two backgrounds visible. We will create a room and enable the user to control the player object using the arrow keys on the keyboard. The player should follow the direction of the arrow keys pressed by the user. Let's first create an object called `player` by clicking on the Add an Object icon in the Main Toolbar. In the dialog box that appears, let's rename the object to be known as player by editing the textbox labeled Name in the upper-left corner of the Properties window as shown in Figure 5.2. Let's also assign the sprite named `player_left` to this object. This is done by left-clicking in the text box beneath the box labeled Sprite as shown in Figure 5.2. This will result in a pop-up menu with all the possible sprites you can use. Choosing one of the items in the list will make the selected sprite active for the object.

FIGURE 5.2   Loading a sprite into an object.

We are now ready to build some intelligence into this object. Let's think of how this object will react to external events. We want this object to do four simple things in response to external events. They are listed in the following Table 5.2.

TABLE 5.2

External Event	Action to Perform
User presses the up arrow	Move the object up 5 pixels
User presses the down arrow	Move the object down 5 pixels
User presses the left arrow	Move the object left 5 pixels
User presses the right arrow	Move the object right 5 pixels

Now let's look at how to set these behaviors for the object. In Game Maker, objects respond to external events by executing different actions. It is up to the game designer to design what events an object responds to and what action it performs when that event occurs. Looking back at Figure 2.17 in Chapter 2, notice that the properties sheet for every object has three areas that are used to customize the object's behavior.

The Active Events Area is in the center of the properties sheet and it is empty to start with. This area holds all the events the object responds to. The Actions Area holds all of the actions that are performed when an event occurs. Clicking on an event in the Events Area will result in the display of all the actions that will be performed for that event. Several actions could be performed when an event occurs. All the actions that could be performed are listed in the Actions Library Area. They are grouped by functionality in tabbed panes. Clicking on the name of the pane on the right activates it and makes it possible to choose actions in that tab. The Add Event button lists all the events that could be added to the Active Events Area.

Clicking on the Add Event button in the Object Properties dialog box opens up the Events Selector Menu. Most of the items in this menu have more subselections that are listed as pop-up menus once again. Now click on the Add Event button and then click on the Keyboard event. We should see all the selections available under it, as shown in Figure 5.3.

In the menu that pops up, let's choose the item labeled Left by left-clicking on it. The event is immediately added to

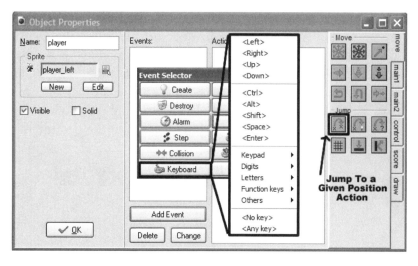

FIGURE 5.3 Keyboard event details.

the Active Events Area. At this point, the object knows it has to look out for any keyboard events where the left arrow is pressed. Our next job is to tell the object what to do when it encounters a left cursor keyboard event. We do this by clicking on an action in the Action Library area and dragging it into the Active Actions Area. In our case we want the object to move left when the user presses the left arrow on the keyboard. Several actions in the library area could be used for this purpose, but we will choose the action called Jump to a Given Position that is found on the move pane, as shown in Figure 5.3. Let's click on the Jump to a Given Position icon in the Actions Area and then drag it to the Active Actions Area and drop it there. As soon as you drop it, you should see the Property box for the action displayed. In our case, it is the Jump to a Given Position Property box shown in Figure 5.4.

This property box asks for an input that could be used to move the object. When the left arrow is pressed on the keyboard, we want the object to move left. The easiest way to move an object left is to move it a few pixels to the left. We can do this by entering a value of –5 for the X value and 0 for the Y value. We want the object to move five pixels relative to where it was, so we need to also check the Relative Check box, as shown in Figure 5.4. If we do not check the Relative box at the bottom, the action would result in moving the object to the absolute X and Y positions. An absolute value of (−5,0) would move the object to the top-left corner of the game room.

The action we created applies to the current object only, so let's leave the Applies To selection at the default value of

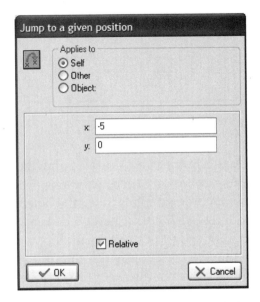

FIGURE 5.4 Jump to a Given Position action.

Self. Click on the OK button to close the properties box. We have now completed assigned actions that have to be completed when the left arrow key on the keyboard is pressed.

Next we need to add events for the right, up, and down arrow keys and assign appropriate actions to each of them.

For the Keyboard > Right event, we want the object to move to a position (5,0) relative to where it was. Let's click on the Add Event button and choose Keyboard > Right. The event is added to the Active Events Area. Now let's drag the Jump to Given Position action to the Active Actions Area.

Let's set the values of X and Y to 5 and 0, respectively, and be sure to check the Relative button, also. Clicking the OK button will add the second Event-Action pair for our object.

Similarly, let's add the Keyboard > Up event to our active events list and the Jump to Given Position action to the active actions list. The X and Y values should be set to 0 and –5, respectively. Moving an object –5 pixels in the Y direction makes it move upward. Let's once again remember to set the Relative Check box. Clicking the OK button will add the third event the object can respond to.

We need to repeat the procedure for the fourth time to handle the down arrow. The values to set X and Y in the Jump to Given Position Properties box should be set to 0 and 5, and do not forget what we need to do with the Relative Check box at the bottom.

At the end of all this, we have given instructions to our object to respond to four separate events by moving in four different directions. The Object Properties box should look like that shown in Figure 5.5.

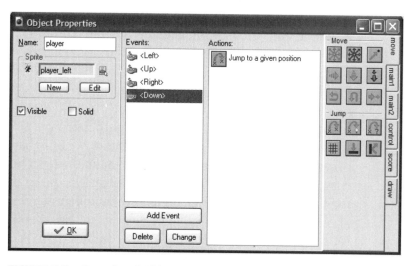

FIGURE 5.5 Completed Object Properties box.

If you want to make any corrections to the actions assigned to a certain event, you need to first left-click on that selected event in the Active Events Area. Doing so will display the list of actions assigned to the selected event in the Active Actions Area. Each of these actions could be modified by double-clicking on the action. The properties sheet for the action is displayed. Modifications made here will be reflected the next time the game runs. If an action is to be deleted, you could right-click on the action and then choose the delete option.

After all the events have been assigned to actions, we could close the Object Properties box by left-clicking on the OK button. We are now ready to place this object in a room and see what it does.

ADDING A ROOM

We now have an object that will respond and move according to the cursor key commands from a keyboard. Let's create a room and place this object in the room and then test the game. To add a new room, click on the Add a Room icon in the Main Toolbar. You will see the Room Properties dialog window on your screen. On the righthand side of the Room Properties window is a grid in dark gray. This is the Workspace of the room where object can be placed. Left-clicking on the Object Selection icon (see Figure 2.13) provides us with a list of objects we could select. Since we only have the player object in our game so far, we make this selection by left-clicking on it. We can place the object in our room by left-clicking in the Workspace, as shown in Figure 5.6.

We can now see how the player object behaves in our room by clicking on the Run Game icon the Main Toolbar. Try moving the player object using the cursor keys. It should move in the direction of the cursor keys you pressed. If it moves in the wrong direction, it is most likely that you set the actions to have incorrect X and Y values. If the player jumps to the top left corner, you may have missed setting the relative option in the Jump To Position Properties box. A working version of the example we have created is available in the directory Chapter5\Example5.2.gm6 on your CD-ROM.

ON THE CD

Congratulations! We can now make an object take commands from the keyboard.

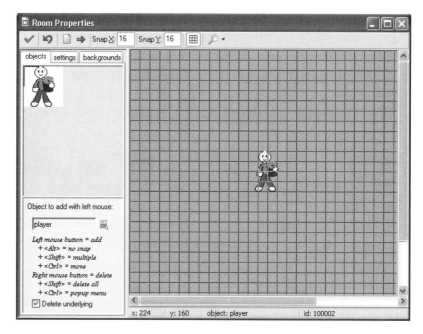

FIGURE 5.6   Room with `player` object. Courtesy of Ramya Swamy. Reprinted with permission.

MODIFYING THE OBJECT'S APPEARANCE

Let's tweak the game a little and make the player point in the direction it is moving. This will make it more realistic when we use the repellant to ward off the bugs. We will use the space bar to make the player shoot bug-spray. Thus, if we are heading to the left and we press the space bar, we would like the spray to discharge toward the left. To do that, we need to change the orientation of the sprite to be in the direction we are heading.

Let's continue with the game created earlier in this chapter. You can load Chapter5\Example5.2.gm6 from the CD-ROM to proceed. You should be at a point where you have control over the player and are able to move it in different directions using the arrow keys.

Let's make some changes to the property of the player object. The easiest way to see the properties of the object is to double-click the `player` object in the Resource Explorer. You should see the familiar events that you added earlier and the actions associated with each of the events.

We will now add an additional action when the arrow keys are pressed. This action will switch the sprite attached to the object. If the event received by the `player` object is a left keyboard event, we want the object to display the sprite pointing to the left. Similarly, we would like to do the same for the three other keyboard events our object responds to.

Let's click on the Left event in the Active Events Area and see what actions are associated with it. You may notice that there is only one action, the `Jump to Position` action. In the Action Library Panel, let's click on the Main1 tab, as shown in Figure 5.7.

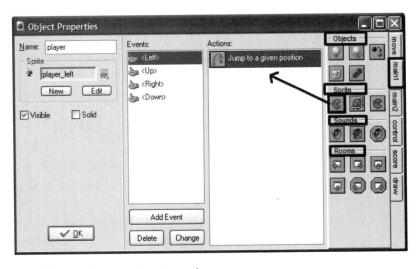

FIGURE 5.7 Change Sprite action.

This should display all of the actions that are categorized into four subpanels on the righthand side of the Object Properties box. The four subpanels are labeled as follows: Objects, Sprite, Sounds, and Rooms. Actions found under each subpanel provide functionality that is closely related. For example, there are three actions under the Sprite subpanel. The first one allows you to change the sprite, the second one allows you to transform the sprite, and the third one allows you to blend the sprite. You can get the help tool tip to display by positioning your mouse over each of these icons for a few seconds.

We would like to change the sprite displayed when different cursor keys are pressed, so let's drag and drop the Change the Sprite icon from the Action Library into the Active Actions Area. You should see a dialog box that allows you to customize the action's default characteristics. Every time you add an action to an object's Active Action list, you can modify certain default characteristics of the action. In the case of the action associated with the left cursor key keyboard event, we need to change the sprite to `player_left`. Once that is done, we can close the Properties box by clicking on the OK button.

We need to repeat this procedure for the remaining three keyboard events this object responds to. This will result in the object executing two actions for the up, down, left, and right keyboard events it encounters. The first action will be to move the object and the second one will be to change the sprite to point in the appropriate direction. Add actions to the remaining three keyboard events as follows (Table 5.3):

TABLE 5.3

Event	Action to Add
Right	Change sprite to player_right
Up	Change sprite to player_up
Down	Change sprite to player_down

Now test the game. You should see the `player` object changing its shape every time you move in a different direction. Save the game in your own folder using the name Example 5.3.

Congratulations! You now know how to control the appearance of objects.

SUMMARY

In this chapter we built a game that exterminates bugs. We created a game room and learned to control and move an object using the cursor keys on the keyboard. We also dynamically changed the appearance of the object by replacing the underlying sprite whenever the user presses a different cursor key, and created new rooms and placed objects in the room.

Projects

As an exercise try to move an object controlled by the keyboard using the *Start Moving in a Direction* action. The example we showed in this chapter used the *Jump to a Given Position* action. Now, what happens when you place two instances of the object controlled by the keyboard in the game room? They should both move and respond to the same set of external events and execute the same actions.

CHAPTER 6

Creating Projectiles

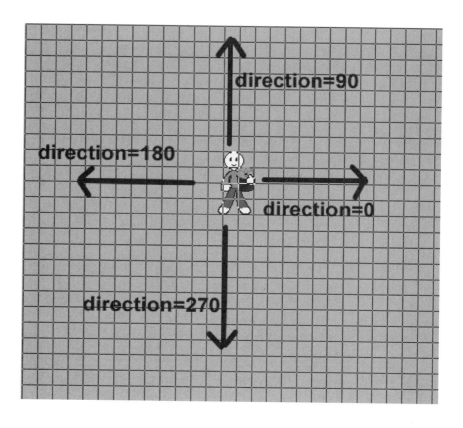

In this chapter:

- Opening Previous Work
- Projectile Dynamics
- Using Variables
- Creating the Projectile
- Launching the Projectile
- Saving Completed Work

In the earlier chapters, we learned how to control objects by using the keyboard and how to change an object's appearance on the fly. Now let's look into the mechanism used to create projectiles, which in general are objects that follow a trajectory based on certain laws of physics.

OPENING PREVIOUS WORK

ON THE CD You could either open up the file you saved at the end of Chapter 5 or use the supplied Game Maker file found in \Chapter6\Example6.0.gm6 to get started with this chapter. It has a couple of sprites and backgrounds that we created earlier and allows you to control the `player` object using the keyboard arrow keys.

PROJECTILE DYNAMICS

Most games have some form of projectiles—either bullets, missiles, magic potions, bombs, arrows, or some other object that provides a means of defense for the player. The projectile is meant to keep enemies away and in some cases destroy them. All projectiles in real life follow the laws of physics. They start moving with an initial speed in a specific direction (*initial velocity*) and follow a trajectory that is influenced by external forces. Projectiles have a finite lifetime that is defined as the period from when they were activated to the time they are destroyed. We can define two key events that happen in their lifetime: a `Create` event and a `Destroy` event. The projectile receives a `Create` event when it is activated and it receives the `Destroy` event when it either explodes or its life comes to an end. All game objects utilize these two events. They receive a `Create` event when they are born and they receive a `Destroy` event when they are about to die. Many objects receive the `Create` event when the game starts or when the room in which they are present is loaded. Objects receive the `Destroy` event when their lifetimes come to an end or when the game ends.

In our game, we are going to create a projectile every time the spacebar is pressed. The projectile is going to be a self-contained Game Maker object that has special characteristics. When this object receives the `Create` event, it is going to start moving in a certain direction. We will set an internal timer within this object so that it destroys itself after one second. The user playing the game will see a cloud of bug-spray emitted near the player as soon as the spacebar is pressed. This spray object is our projectile. It will start moving with an initial velocity of five pixels per step as soon as it is created. It will also set an internal alarm so that it can be notified after one second has elapsed. The game engine generates an `Alarm` event at the end of the one-second period. When the object receives this `Alarm` event, it destroys itself. The user will see the player emitting fumes from the repellant can when the user presses the spacebar. These fumes will start moving and will disappear after one second.

USING VARIABLES

We can keep track of the direction in which the player object is moving by using a variable. *Variables* are storage locations where you can store information. Each storage location has a name associated with it. The contents of the storage location can be retrieved and replaced by using the storage location's name. This name is referred to as the variable's name. Let's create a variable on the player object and name it `direction`.

The player can move in different directions that are defined by an angle that can be anywhere from 0 to 360 degrees. A player moving at an angle of zero moves to the right. An angle of 90 degrees moves the player up, an angle of 180 degrees moves the player to the left, and an angle of 270 degrees moves the player down, as shown in Figure 6.1. These four values are what we will be using in our game. You could use other values to move in other directions. For example, an angle of 45 degrees will move the player toward the top-right corner.

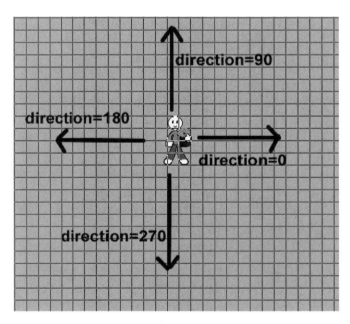

FIGURE 6.1   Defining the angles for the direction variable.
Images courtesy of Ramya Swamy. Reprinted with permission.

Let's create the direction variable in the `Create` event for the `player` object and set its value to zero. This defines the default direction of motion to be to the right. To add the Create event, click on the Add Event button on the player object's property box. Variables are created using the Set the Variable action in last row of the Control tab of the Action Library. It is the first action under the variables subpanel of the Control tab. Next let's drag and drop the Set Variable action and set its values, as shown in Figure 6.2.

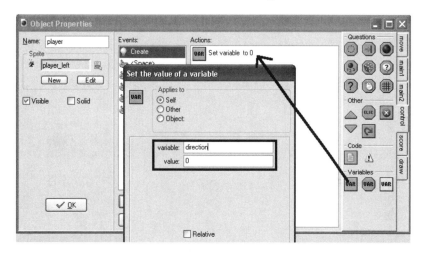

FIGURE 6.2   Set the direction variable in the Create event.

Let's also fill up the direction variable with an appropriate angle based on the direction of motion shown in Figure 6.2. These values reflect the direction in which the player object is moving. The following Table 6.1 shows the direction of motion and the values of the direction variable.

TABLE 6.1

Direction of Motion	Value of Direction Variable
Left	180
Right	0
Up	90
Down	270

From Table 6.1, we know that the direction variable has a value of 90 if the player object is moving up. We now need to add the Set the Variable action for the player object's keyboard events left, right, up, and down to reflect the direction in which the player is moving.

Let's next select the Left keyboard event in the player object's properties window. There should be two actions present there already. Let's now add the Set the Variable action by dragging and dropping it from the Action library onto the Active Actions Area. In the Set the Variable Properties box, set the name of the variable to direction and the value to 180, as shown in Figure 6.3. Click the OK button to accept the change.

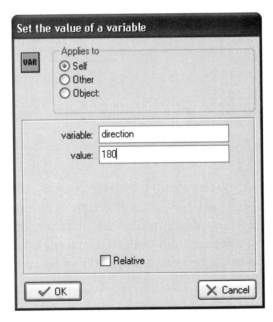

FIGURE 6.3   Set the Variable Property box.

You should now see that the Left keyboard event has three actions associated with it. The third action is the one we just added. This new action sets the variable named direction with a value of 180. The up, down, and right keyboard events have to be modified to include the Set the Variable action to set the values to 90, 270, and 0 respectively. The `direction` variable defines the direction in which the spray object should travel.

Add the Set the Variable action to the left, right, up, and down keyboard events handled by the `player` object. The action list for the down arrow is shown as an example in Figure 6.4. The `player` object now keeps track of the direction in which it is moving. We will use this information to set the direction in which the `SprayObject` will move in once it is created.

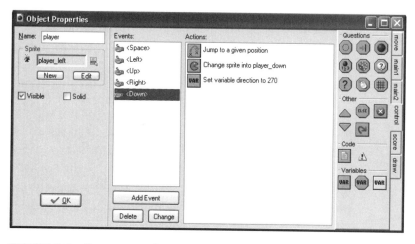

FIGURE 6.4   Down cursor key Event Action list.

CREATING THE PROJECTILE

In this game, a spray object will be our projectile. The spray will be discharged from the repellant can held by the player when the spacebar is pressed. Let's first create a sprite for the spray object. You can create a sprite that is the default 32×32 pixels in size. Using the spray can in the image editor, create a small blob of white fog in the center of the sprite, as shown in Figure 6.5. Rename the sprite `Spray`.

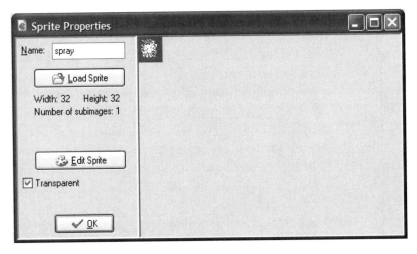

FIGURE 6.5 Spray sprite.

Let's create an object called SprayObject that uses the Spray sprite. Note that the Active Events list is always empty to start with. Now let's configure the SprayObject to behave like a projectile. This object is not programmed to respond to any events initially. The first event we want the SprayObject to respond to is the Create event, so let's add the Create event to the Active Events list, as shown in Figure 6.6.

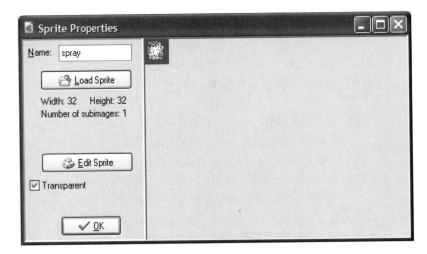

FIGURE 6.6 Create event for SprayObject.

The only action we will be performing for the `Create` event is to set an alarm. We will be using an alarm to help set the life of the projectile. Setting an alarm generates an `Alarm` event at the end of the defined period.

The `Set an Alarm Clock` action is found under the Timings subpanel of the Main2 tab of the Actions Library. Drag and drop it into the Active Actions Area. In the Properties box for this action, set the number of steps to 30 and leave everything else at their default values, as shown in Figure 6.6. Close the Alarm Clock dialog box by clicking on the OK button.

Now let's add an `Alarm0` event to the Active Events list for this spray object and add the `Destroy` action from the Main1 tab of the Action Library for this event. For the `Destroy` action we can leave everything at the default values. The completed object properties sheet for the `SprayObject` will look like that shown in Figure 6.7

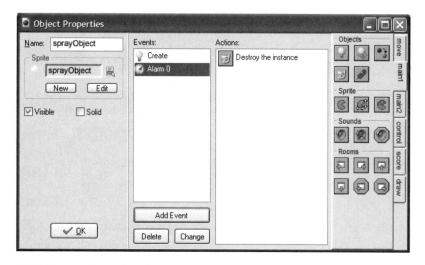

FIGURE 6.7 Completed `SprayObject`.

LAUNCHING THE PROJECTILE

We now have the SprayObject configured correctly to be our projectile and we know the direction in which the SprayObject should travel when it is created. Let's launch a projectile when the spacebar is pressed.

We will use the Keyboard spacebar event in the player object to trigger the launch of the SprayObject (the projectile). This may sound confusing, but once we start doing the real task, it will become simple to understand. Let's first display the properties of the player object by double-clicking on the Player icon in the Resource Explorer. We have the player object responding to four keys of the keyboard. Let's also make it respond to the spacebar. To do this, add a Keyboard event for the spacebar just like you did for the cursor keys. The spacebar is named Space in the pop-up menu for the Keyboard event.

When the player receives a Keyboard spacebar event, let's execute an action that creates a spray object with motion. This is done by dragging and dropping the Create an Instance Of an Object with Motion action from the Main1 tab of the Actions Library, as shown in Figure 6.8.

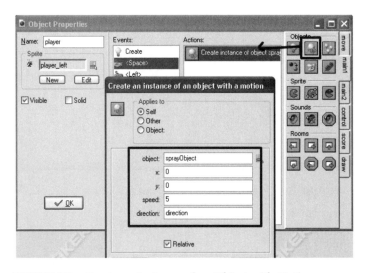

FIGURE 6.8 Create an Instance of an Object with Motion Properties box.

The action that looks like a yellow light bulb with a red arrow is the one we need to drag and drop. In the Properties box for this action, the first choice asks you to choose the object that we want to set in motion. We need to choose the SprayObject as the object that will start moving like a projectile. The next two fields define the location from which this object will start moving. Let's leave both these values at zero and check the Relative box at the bottom of this properties window. Value of zero for the X and Y fields will define the starting location of the projectile to be at the same location as that of the player (a distance of zero from the player). Let's set the speed to five pixels per step.

We defined the direction variable earlier. It holds the direction of motion for the SprayObject. Let's type in the name of the variable direction in the Direction field, as shown in Figure 6.8.

Before you close the Properties box shown in Figure 6.8, be sure to check the following settings: The Object field should be set to SprayObject, the X and Y values should be set to zero, the speed should be set to five pixels per step, the direction variable should be set to direction, and most importantly, the Relative box should be checked.

At this point, we have the player object in a position to create a SprayObject when the spacebar is pressed. When the SprayObject is created, it knows in which direction it should move.

SAVING COMPLETED WORK

It is time to save the work done in this chapter as Chapter6Final in the directory of your choice. We have provided a completed example that lists all the work we have done until now. The competed example is available in the file Examples\Chapter6\Example6.1.gm6. The game assets we have created so far are listed below in Table 6.2:

TABLE 6.2

Asset Type	Asset Name
Sprites	player_left, player_right, player_down, player_up
Backgrounds	grass, title screen
Object	player, spray
Rooms	room1

Our game at this point has a `player` object that can move around and launch `SprayObjects`. The `SprayObjects` have finite lifetimes and move in specified directions at specified speeds before they self-destruct. We have made exceptional progress creating the infrastructure for our game so far. Now we'll proceed to use our `SprayObject` for useful purposes and add an element of danger to the game to make it more interesting.

SUMMARY

In this chapter, we learned to create projectiles such as bullets, missiles, and magic potions. Remember that projectiles start with a defined speed and have a finite lifetime. They use the `Create Event` to start moving at a certain speed and use an alarm event to self-destruct.

We learned about the importance of variables and what they could be used for. In the example we used a variable to hold the direction of motion. We looked at the various actions that use variables in the `Control Tab`.

We also looked at using the `Alarm Event` and learned to create instances of objects using the `Create an Instance Of an Object` action.

Project

1) Try to make the player shoot water when the W key is pressed. The water should shoot in the direction the player is moving. Make the water travel further than the aerosol spray object, which may require you to use a larger Alarm interval to achieve this. 2) You could also create other projectiles that are more powerful and more valuable to the player. Explore the possibility of making these special projectiles available to the player after reaching a certain score.

CHAPTER 7

Incorporating Multiple Levels

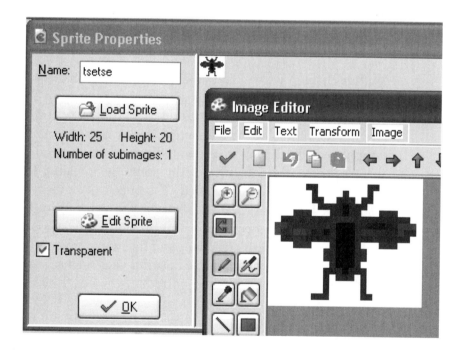

In this chapter:

- Opening Previous Work
- Adding a Background to Our Room
- Creating a Bug Object
- Creating Another Bug Object
- Creating the Swamp
- Additional Events for the Bug Object
- Including Health and Lives
- Incorporating the Score
- Incorporating Multiple Levels
- Adding a New Room
- Adding Sound

In this chapter, we will add objects that give an element of surprise to our game and make interesting game play. We will be creating bug objects that could harm the player and be exterminated by using the bug-spray. The bugs are born in a swamp from which they are generated at random. We will be able to control the difficulty of the game by adjusting the speed at which they are generated. The bugs will be moving around inside the room that we created in the earlier chapters.

You may have noticed that in our previous game, we created just two objects: the repellant and the bug-spray. In this chapter, we will be creating some harmful bugs such as mosquitoes, flies, and more that could reduce the health of the player.

OPENING PREVIOUS WORK

Let's first open the work we have done previously in Game Maker. You could alternatively open the file provided in CD-ROM from Chapter7\Example7.1.gm6. It has two objects: the player and the spray object.

ADDING A BACKGROUND TO OUR ROOM

Let's explore the Background and the Room assets we have by expanding these two folders in the Game Maker Resource Explorer Window. You will see two backgrounds that we created: the title screen and grass. We have only one room, called room1, so far. Let's open the properties sheet for room1 by double-clicking on room1 in the Resource Explorer window of Game Maker. In the properties sheet of room1, click on the Backgrounds tab and then click on the location shown in Figure 7.1. From the pop-up menu, choose grass to be the image of your choice. By default, the image now becomes the new background image and it should completely fill up the room. The room should now have a whole new grassy look.

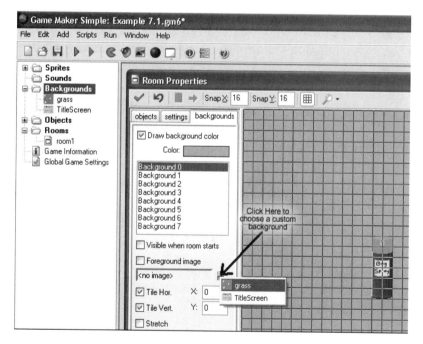

FIGURE 7.1 Backgrounds property sheet.

CREATING A BUG OBJECT

We need to create several types of bugs that are born in a swamp. We'll start by creating an African tsetse (pronounced see-see) fly. The tsetse fly is slightly larger than a horse fly and it is found in Africa. Tsetse flies are hard to control, and tsetse fly infestation is becoming more and more serious in Africa. A tsetse fly can drink twice its weight in blood at every meal and can cause sleeping sickness. In our game, if this bug bites us, we will loose health.

Let's first create the sprite for the tsetse fly. Add a new sprite, name it tsetseSprite, and create an image using the Image Editor that looks something like that shown in Figure 7.2. The image should be about 25 pixels wide and 20 pixels high. It may take you a couple of minutes to perfect it and get it to look the way you want it to. That's OK. If you prefer, you could always load the image of the tsetse fly provided on the CD-ROM that accompanies this book. You will find that picture under the following filename: Resources\sprites\ tsetse.bmp.

ON THE CD

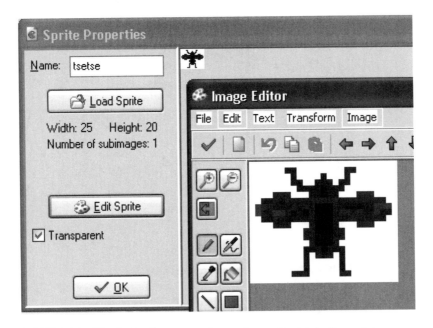

FIGURE 7.2 The tsetse fly. Courtesy of Ramya Swamy. Reprinted with permission.

The tsetse flies in real life live only for about six to ten weeks. In our game, we'll let them have a life span of six to ten seconds. We'll also have them evolve from the swamp at a rate of two every five seconds. The tsetse flies will start moving in a random direction at a speed of four pixels per step.

We shall now proceed to create the tsetse object. Create a new object, called `tsetseObject` and assign the tsetse sprite to this object. Next, add a `Create` event and an action to make the object move in a random direction with a speed of four pixels per step, as shown in Figure 7.3. Clicking on all the eight arrows designating the different directions of motion shown in Figure 7.3 makes the object move in a random direction. We'll also set an alarm for eight seconds (eight seconds is $8 \times 30 = 240$ steps), as shown in Figure 7.4. The Set an Alarm Action icon is on the top-left corner of the Main2 tab. We have used alarms in other parts of the game, so be sure to use Alarm #2 for this step. Setting an alarm will generate an `Alarm` event that we will design in the next few steps. When the `Alarm` event occurs, we'll destroy the tsetse fly. For the player of the game, it will seem as though the tsetse fly lived for eight seconds and then died.

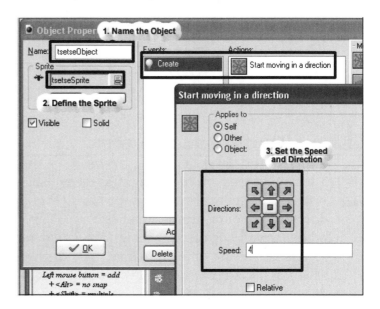

FIGURE 7.3 Create event.

The `Alarm` action we used in Figure 7.4 generates an `Alarm` event. We will handle the `Alarm` event by clicking on the Add Event button to add an `Alarm` Event Handler for Alarm #2. Let's also add an action to destroy the instance and leave the default setting for the destroy action. The `Alarm` event and the `Destroy` action are shown in Figure 7.5. Our tsetse fly object is now ready. If an instance of this object is created, it moves around in a random direction and gets destroyed after eight seconds. We can now close the Object Properties window for the tsetse object.

FIGURE 7.4   Adding the `Alarm` action.

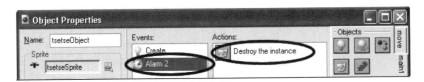

FIGURE 7.5   Adding the `Alarm` Event Handler.

CREATING ANOTHER BUG OBJECT

ON THE CD

You could create one more object by using the sprite designated dogtick.bmp provided on the CD-ROM in the sprites directory (Resources\sprites\dogtick.bmp). This depicts another harmful bug called the dog tick. Follow the same instructions but use different parameters for the alarm, the length of life, and the speed at which it moves to create the dog tick.

CREATING THE SWAMP

We have at least one bug object at this point and we can now start a swamp that generates tsetse flies. Let's create a sprite that represents a swamp by adding a new sprite and naming it swamp. Let's edit this blank sprite using the Image Editor to create a swamp-like image similar to the one shown in Figure 7.6. A size of 32 pixels by 32 pixels would be appropriate for the swamp sprite.

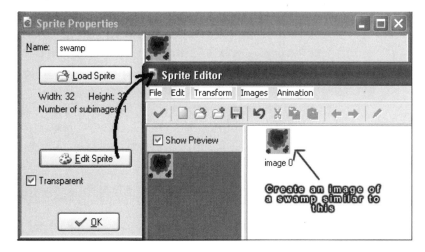

FIGURE 7.6 The swamp sprite.

You can also create the image using an external image editing application and then import it into Game Maker's Sprite Editor.

With a swamp sprite in place, we can start creating the swamp object. Create a new object and name it SwampObject. Assign the swamp sprite you created in the previous step to this object.

It is time to start thinking about the behaviors to add for this new object. The SwampObject is one from which harmful insects are born. To simulate the swamp behavior, we will be setting an internal alarm that is generated randomly within the SwampObject. Whenever an Alarm event occurs, a bug will be created. After the first Alarm event occurs, if we want more Alarm events to be generated at periodic intervals, we need to reset the alarm.

We can use a mathematical function provided by Game Maker for generating alarms at different intervals of time. The function random needs a numerical argument provided to it. It then generates a random number that is anywhere from zero to that number. For example, if we use the function random(30), Game Maker generates a random number that is anywhere between 0 and 30.

Let's make things simple and instead add an alarm that will occur every second. We can start by adding behaviors for the SwampObject. The SwampObject will have a lifecycle similar to the game room in which it is placed. We'll first add the Create event and add an action to set Alarm #1. All four steps described so far and the properties for the Alarm action are shown in Figure 7.7. The four steps to complete are:

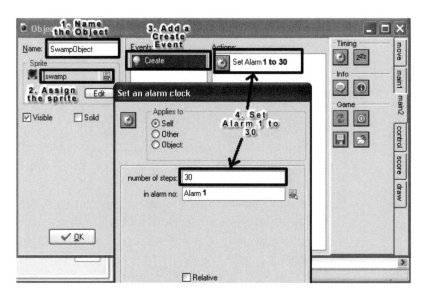

FIGURE 7.7 Create event for the SwampObject.

1. Name the object.
2. Assign the sprite.
3. Add a Create event.
4. Add an action to set Alarm #1 o 30 (steps).

Next let's work on making the Alarm event occur repeatedly. Add an Alarm#1 event by clicking on the Add Event button, as shown in Figure 7.8. There are a couple of actions to add to this event. We want to create a tsetseObject every second from the swamp. To do this, choose the Main2 tab of the Action Library and click and drag the Create Instance of an Object icon to create an instance of the tsetse fly object. Make sure that the Relative button is checked in the Create Instance Action's properties box or else you will see the tsetseObject created at the top-left corner of the screen. After creating the instance of the tsetse fly, we need to reset the alarm so that the tsetse flies can be generated at variable intervals of time. Use the Set an Alarm Clock action from the Main2 tab, type in the value 30, and choose the Set Alarm#1 action again. The two actions associated with the Alarm event are shown in Figure 7.8.

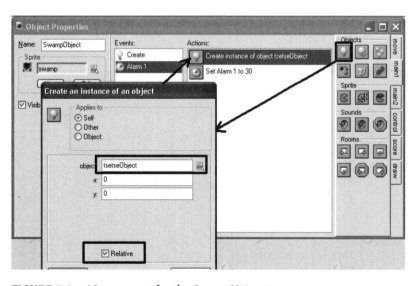

FIGURE 7.8 Alarm event for the SwampObject.

We next need to next place the SwampObject in our first
game room. This is done by double-clicking on the room1 (or
room0) selection in the Rooms folder of the Resource Explorer. Let's click on the Object Selection icon (shown in Figure 2.13) and choose the swampObject. Now left-click inside
the room to place an instance of the SwampObject, as shown
in Figure 7.9.

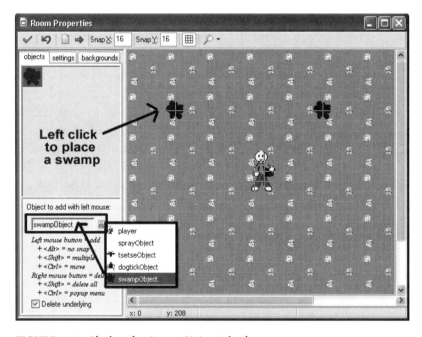

FIGURE 7.9   Placing the SwampObject in the room.

ADDITIONAL EVENTS FOR THE BUG OBJECT

Let's take a moment to play the game in its current state. You
may immediately notice that you cannot kill the bugs with
the bug repellant. We can fix that problem by adding an additional Collision event for the different bug objects. If the
bug collides with the spray object, let the bug destroy itself.
To the player of the game, it will seem as though the bug-

spray killed the bug. Open the properties sheet for the `tset-seObject` and click on Add Event to add a `Collision` event with the `sprayObject`. In the Actions Area, choose the Destroy Instance icon found under the Main1 tab of the Action Library. Drag and drop the Destroy Instance into the active Actions Area. Leave the default setting for the `Destroy` action so that the object destroys itself. The completed Collision Handler is shown in Figure 7.10.

FIGURE 7.10 Collision Event Handler.

We defined the duration of life for the `tsetseObject` to be eight seconds. However, the `tsetseObject` may leave the boundary of the room well before eight seconds. Since we do not have a wall restricting the movement of the bugs, we'll make the objects return to their starting point if they move outside the room. We'll add an event handler to take care of these `Outside Room` events. This event is generated when the object leaves the defined boundary of the room. Let's add an `Outside Room` event to the `tsetseObject` by clicking on the Add Event button, as shown in Figure 7.11. The `Outside Room` event is found under the Other menu button in the Event Selector pop-up menu. When this event happens, we would like to move the bug back inside the room so it can continue to live the rest of its life. Let's programmatically move the bug back to the place it was born by dragging the `Jump to Start Position` action found under the Move Action tab in the Action Library window into the Active Actions list.

The completed list of actions required to move the `tsetseObjects` outside the room back to the swamp is shown in Figure 7.11

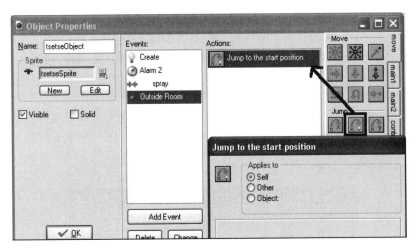

FIGURE 7.11   Outside the Room Handler.

You can also use the Jump to a Given Position action to achieve the same purpose, but you'll need to specify the exact coordinates of the destination. The coordinates of an object are defined by using a .x or a .y suffix to the name of the object, so the coordinates of the swamp object are defined by the definitions SwampObject.x and SwampObject.y. We'll use these two values to make the tsetse fly object jump back to the swamp if it leaves the room. Since the Jump to Start Position action does not require that you type in any values, we'll use it, as shown in Figure 7.11.

The Game Completed until this point can be found in the file Chapter7\Example7.4.gm6.

ON THE CD

INCLUDING HEALTH AND LIVES

Now that we have dangerous bugs being generated from the swamp, let's add different degrees of health and lives into the game to keep the players excited. In Game Maker, the health and lives action provided in the Action Library refers to the health and the lives of the player. In our case, the player is the bug repellant that we control to kill the bugs. We'll start the player with three lives and 100% health. This means that every time a bug bites the player, the player's health will be reduced by 10%. A player with no health left looses one life, and when there are no more lives left, the game will terminate. To incorporate this new feature, we need to add logic that sets and manipulates the player's health. The ideal place to initialize health and lives for the player would be when the player is created (or born). This would be in response to the `Create` Event for the player object. The health and lives of the player could also be reduced in response to a collision event with the `tsetseObject`. Choose the player object by double-clicking on it in the Resource Explorer. Table 7.1 shows the additional events to add to the player object and a description of the actions that will be performed in response these events.

TABLE 7.1

Event	Actions
`Create` event	Set health to 100, set lives to 3, Set window caption information
Collision with `tsetseFly`	Reduce health by 10; destroy the other object
No more health	Reduce lives by 1; Set health to 100
No more lives	Display message; end game

The `No More Health` and `No More Lives` events are found in the Other section of the Event Selector pop-up window. The various lives and health action icons are found under the Score tab of the Action Library.

Figure 7.12 shows the `Create` event and the associated actions for the repellant object. Figure 7.13 shows the actions executed when the Collision Handler invoked. Two actions are executed when a collision occurs. The first one reduces the health and the second one destroys the other object.

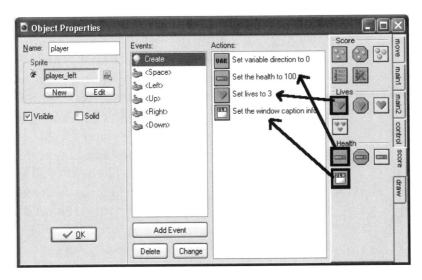

FIGURE 7.12 Create Event Handler.

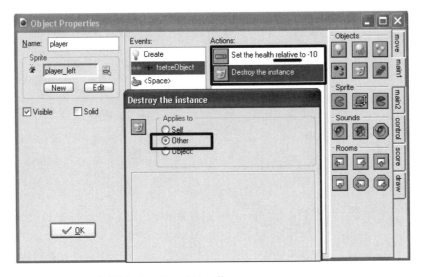

FIGURE 7.13 Collision Event Handler.

Incorporate the events and actions shown in Figure 7.14, which shows the Event Handler for the No More Health event, and Figure 7.15, which shows the Event Handler for the No More Lives event. Verify that you have all the events and actions shown in Figures 7.12, 7.13, 7.14, and 7.15.

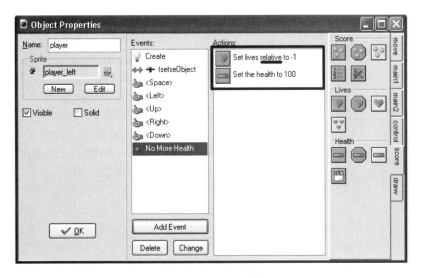

FIGURE 7.14   No More Health Event Handler.

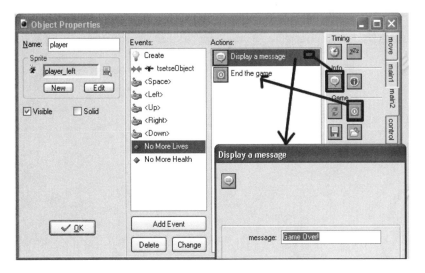

FIGURE 7.15   No More Lives Event Handler.

For an example of the game completed until this point, go to the CD-ROM and take a look at the file entitled Chapter7\Example7.5.gm6.

INCORPORATING THE SCORE

We now need to incorporate the addition of score for the game. Let's award the players 20 points for every bug that is killed. This can be done when the tsetseObject collides with the sprayObject. Let's add the Set the Score action to the Collision event, as shown in Figure 7.16. Make sure that you check the Relative checkbox in the Set the Score properties sheet. Otherwise your score will not increase beyond the set value of 20 points!

Now let's play the game. Every time you kill a bug, you should see your score rise by 20 points. The game has been relatively easy so far, and this is to encourage novice players to want to continue playing the game. Now let's raise the stakes and take the player to a whole new level of difficulty after they reach a score of 200 points. We will do this by incorporating new rooms.

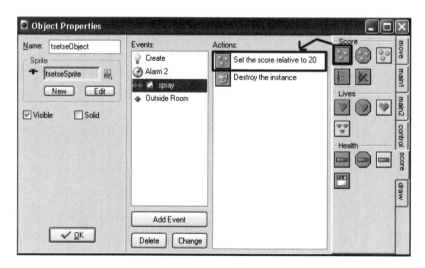

FIGURE 7.16   Adding score.

INCORPORATING MULTIPLE LEVELS

ON THE CD
Levels are different rooms the user traverses during game play. The game provided on the CD-ROM in the file Chapter7\example7.6.gm6 incorporates all of the topics we have covered so far. Let's embark upon adding new levels. For this, we'll need a manager object for each room, whose function is to manage all of the activity in that room. This activity includes the logic required to take the user to a new room, such as the command to proceed to the next room after the score reaches 200 points. More complicated logic can be incorporated into the manager object if desired. The manager object typically uses a step event to periodically check if the conditions are right to advance to the next room. It's usually best to keep the manager object invisible to the game player. This can be done either by not assigning a sprite to the manager object or by making the object invisible by clicking on the Visible flag in the Manager Objects property box.

Let's create a manager object and add a step event. Let the first action the manager object performs should be a check to see if the score is greater than 200 points. This action is found under the Score Tab in the Action Library. The next action we will be using will take us to the next room. This action is found under the Main1 tab. Let's drag and drop the Move to Next Room Action into our Active Actions list. When moving from one room to another, it's possible to incorporate different types of transitions. You could choose the style you prefer from the options provided in the Move to Next Room properties box. The completed properties sheet for the Room1Manager object is shown in Figure 7.17. Notice that no sprite is associated with this object and the Visible flag is unchecked.

We now have the Room1Manager Object ready. Place this object anywhere in room1 and you will automatically go to the second room after your score is greater than 200. Before you try that, however, you need to add a new room to your game or you will get a Fatal Error message that tells you that you are trying to move to a nonexistent room.

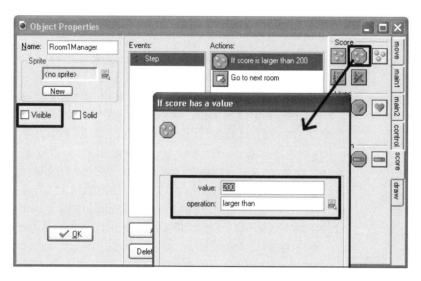

FIGURE 7.17   Room manager properties sheet.

ADDING A NEW ROOM

We now are ready to add a new room to our game. Let's also load the sprites `Bushes`, `WaspHive`, `DogTick`, and `Wasp`, which are found in the Resource/sprites directory of the CD-ROM provided with this book. These sprites will be used to create the objects they refer to. Let's also create empty objects for each of these sprites. Also load a new background—`background2`—from the   Resources/backgrounds directory. The sprites and the associated objects that you need to create are listed in the table shown below. Using the sprites provided, create the four objects listed Table 7.2.

TABLE 7.2

Sprite Name	Object Name
Bushes	bushesObject
DogTick	dogtickObject
WaspHive	hiveObject
Wasp	waspObject

Next click on the Rooms folder to add a new room. Let's also assign the `background2` to the new room. Figure 7.18 depicts all the new assets that we have loaded into our game in preparation for the new level we are working on. At this point, it would be a good idea to meticulously check if all the new assets highlighted in Figure 7.18 are also found in the game you are currently creating.

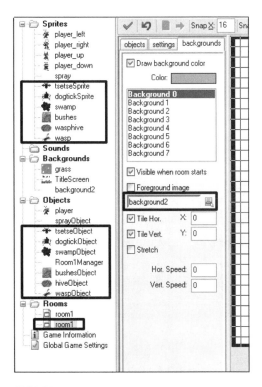

FIGURE 7.18   New game assets.

Now let's provide behaviors for the `dogtickObject` and the `waspObject` so they behave in a similar fashion to the `tsetseObject`. The main difference would be that the `dogtickObject` will be born from bushes and the `waspObject` will emerge from a hive. If a `dogtickObject` bites the player, the player will loose 25 health points. If the `WaspObject` bites the player, 50 health points will be taken away.

The events and actions for the WaspObject are listed in Table 7.3.

TABLE 7.3

Event	Action
Create	Move in random direction with a speed of 10 Set Alarm #2 to 300 steps
Alarm2	Destroy instance (self) Collision (with spray) Add 25 points; set score relative to 25 points Destroy instance (self)
Outside Room	Jump back to start point

The actions and events required for the HiveObject are listed in Table 7.4.

TABLE 7.4

Event	Action
Create	Set Alarm 1 to 60
Alarm1	Create instance of a WaspObject; x = 0; y = 0; Relative = checked Set Alarm 1 to 60

The events and actions for the DogTickObject are listed in Table 7.5.

TABLE 7.5

Event	Action
Create	Move in random direction with a speed of 2 Set Alarm2 to 300 steps
Alarm2	Destroy instance (self) Collision (with spray) Add 15 points by using Set Score Relative 15 Destroy instance (self)
Outside Room	Jump to start position

The actions and events required for the BushObject are listed in Table 7.6.

TABLE 7.6

Event	Action
Create	Set Alarm 1 to 45
Alarm1	Create instance of a dogtickObject; x = 0; y = 0; Relative = checked Set Alarm 1 to 45

We also need to add Collision events when the player object collides with a tickObject or a waspObject. Let's follow the same procedure shown in Figure 7.12 to take care of the Collision event of the payer with the tsetseObject. Activate the player object's Property window by clicking on the player selection in the Resource Explorer. Let's set the properties for the player object as listed in the followng table for the dogtickObject and the waspObject. You can review Figure 7.13, which shows you the actions we used for the Collision event with the tsetseObject (Table 7.7).

TABLE 7.7

Event	Action
Collision with tsetseObject	Reduce health by 10; destroy other (Figure 7.13)
Collision with dogtickObject	Reduce health by 20; Destroy other
Collision with waspObject	Reduce health by 30; destroy other

Let's add the collision with the DogTick first. Click on Add Event and set the actions, as shown in Figure 7.19.

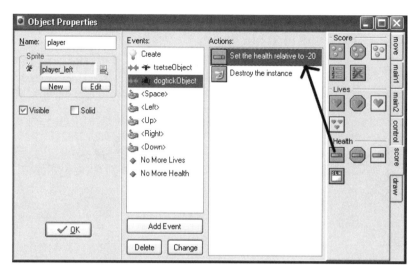

FIGURE 7.19 Collision with `dogtickObject`.

Let's add the collision with the `waspObject` next. Click on Add Event and set the actions, as shown in Figure 7.20.

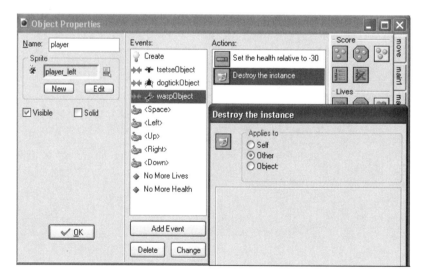

FIGURE 7.20 Collision with `waspObject`.

Now that we have created all the objects we need, it is time to place them in a room and see them interact with each other while the player is controlling the repellant. To place objects in the room, expand the Rooms folder in the Resource Explorer. Double-click on room2 to activate the Room Properties dialog box. Choose the repellant, swamp, hive, and bush objects and place them apart, as shown in Figure 7.21.

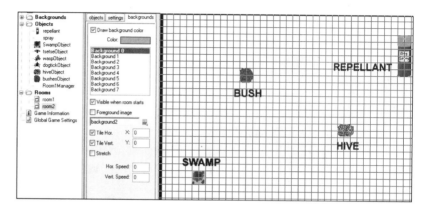

FIGURE 7.21   Room2 populated with objects. Images courtesy of Ramya Swamy. Reprinted with permission.

ON THE CD

The complete game we have created up to this point is available in on the CD-ROM in Chapter7\Example7.7.gm6. Feel free to open it, play it, and examine it. After your score reaches 200 points, you will move from the first level to the next level we just created, but be careful—this new level is a little harder to play since there are more enemies.

ADDING SOUND

Sounds add an extra dimension to the game-playing experience. The sound could be a background music track that plays throughout the game or it could be a small clip played when a certain event occurs. For example, when two objects collide, we could play a sound clip that sounds like a bang. If you have played a traditional game such as *Pacman*, you are familiar with the different kinds of sounds a game can utilize.

Game Maker supports audio files in the wav, wmv, and mp3 formats. In our game, we will play a spray sound when the player presses the spacebar to activate the repellant. We will also use a swat sound whenever a bug is killed. Sound files are loaded using the same mechanism as sprites. Right-click on the Sounds folder in the Resource Explorer and choose Add from the pop-up menu to add a sound. Alternatively, you could click in the Add Menu item and choose the Add Sound menu item or you could click on the Speaker icon the Main Menu bar. The choice is yours. There are a couple of wav files provided in the Resources/Sound directory of the CD-ROM. Several methods can be used to create customized digital music. The easiest method would be to use a microphone and the Microsoft Windows Sound Recorder.

In the Sound Properties box, there are several buttons. Pressing the Load Sound button prompts you with the typical Windows Explorer that allows you to choose the sound file of your choice. After the file is loaded, you can preview the file by pressing on the Green Arrow button next to the Load Sound button. Make sure your speaker is not in the muted mode or else you will not hear anything. It's a good idea to provide a relevant name for the loaded sound. In our case, let's first load the spray sound found in the file Resouces\Sound\spray.wav on the CD-ROM and name it "Spray." Clicking on the OK button finalizes the import process and makes the newly loaded sound file available as a resource to the game. Let's also load the swat sound from the same location and name the sound "Swat."

Let's play the spray sound every time an instance of the SprayObject is created. To do this, double-click on the sprayObject in the Resource Explorer to open up its properties box. Choose the Create event by clicking on it in the events subwindow and prepare to add an additional action that plays a sound clip. The Play a Sound icon is found in the Main1 tab under the Sounds section. Click and drag that onto the Actions subwindow. You will see the properties box for the `Play a Sound` action. Right-clicking on the Text box labeled sound: will prompt you with a pop-up menu with choices, as shown in Figure 7.22. Choose Spray and then click the OK button to close the Sound properties box. You an also close the Spray Objects property box. If you play the game now, you will hear the spray sound every time the space bar is pressed.

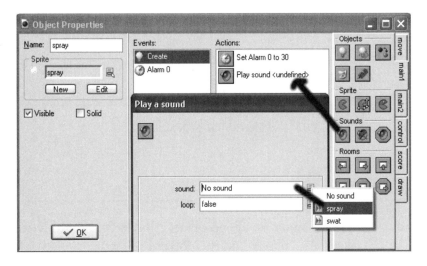

FIGURE 7.22   Adding the spray sound.

In a similar fashion, you need to open up the `tsetseObject`'s property box and add the action to play the swat sound when it collides with the `sprayObject`, as shown in Figure 7.23.

The same thing that was done with the `tsetseObject` needs to be duplicated for the `dogtickObject` and the `waspObject`. Once completed, a swat sound will be generated whenever any of the bug objects collide with a spray object. With the incorporation of the two sound files, the game-playing experience is enriched significantly.

ON THE CD

This concludes our game with bugs. The completed example described in this chapter can be found in CD-ROM at the location Chapter7\Example7.8.gm6.

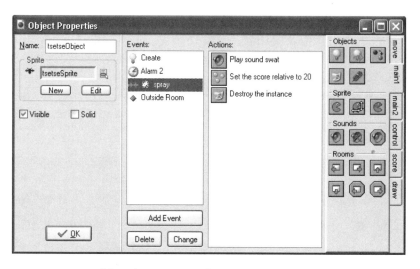

FIGURE 7.23   Adding the swat sound.

SUMMARY

In this chapter we added objects (bugs) that could harm the player. The player had the power to exterminate these bugs by pressing the Spacebar and activating the aerosol can, which sprays in the direction the player is moving and destroys the bugs if it collides with them. We made the mosquitoes spawn from swamps, the bees from hives, and the dog's ticks from bushes. Bugs that left the boundary of the room were brought back magically using the `Jump to Start Position` action. We also used the score, lives, and health actions to display the status and score of the player. And finally we created multiple levels of the game by using more than one game room and incorporated sound into the game.

You also learned that we could use a microphone to create additional sound effects by using the Windows sound recorder utility. The recording utility is found under the windows start menu `WindowsStart->Accessories->Entertainment>SoundRecorder`. Remember to save the files in the WAV format.

Project

1) Make the player move slower if the bugs bite the player. To a game designer this requirement would be translated to the following statement: If the bug collides with the player, reduce the speed of motion and health of the player. 2) You could also create additional game rooms with other enemy objects that are more powerful than those we have created. Exterminating these may require a more powerful projectile.

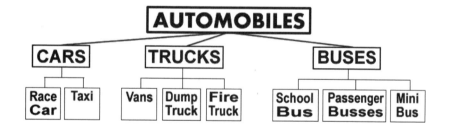

CHAPTER 8

Understanding Inheritance

In this chapter:

- What Is Inheritance?
- Inspecting the DNA Factory Game
- Inspecting the Objects
- Inputting the Common Behavior into a Parent Object

When building object-oriented systems, a designer typically spends substantial time designing the system for efficiency. This is when inefficiencies in the algorithm used to execute different tasks are eliminated. In this chapter, we will be looking at a mechanism used to eliminate repetitive and redundant behavior that is used among a group of related objects. We briefly touched upon the notion of inheritance in earlier chapters, but now we will look at it in-depth using concrete examples.

WHAT IS INHERITANCE?

When designing software systems, it is sometimes possible to find a hierarchical structure with objects. Some objects may behave exactly like one or more other objects in the system and might include additional behaviors. For example, assume we are creating a car racing game. We would need different types of car objects: some would accelerate very fast, some would have automatic gear shifters, and each of them would have different drag coefficients. While designing objects for these cars, it is possible to have different people independently design them. Each person would create behaviors for the car they have been assigned. When all of these objects are put together in the game, we would definitely have a working game. If by chance we needed some additional behaviors incorporated when a very high-octane fuel is used in the car instead of the normal fuel, the car designers would have to redesign their objects to take care of this feature. For example, Let's assume we get an extra 3% power with the use of this new fuel. All of the car objects would have to be redesigned to accelerate and move faster appropriately.

If we had a little foresight and designed the objects using a hierarchical mechanism, we could have saved a lot of time and effort. If we had extracted all of the common features of the cars and created a parent object with those features, it would be easier to make all the changes in one place. All of the special features of each of the cars could have been incorporated into different child objects. We could make each of these child objects inherit features from the parent object. By using a hierarchical object tree like the one shown in Figure 8.1, we could make changes to the parent object to change the behavior of all the child objects.

FIGURE 8.1 Automobile hierarchy diagram. Images courtesy of Ramya Swamy. Reprinted with permission.

To understand how inheritance can be used to make an efficient system, let's look at a game that was designed without much thought to inheritance. It is provided in the CD-ROM that accompanies this book and its complete path is Chapter8\Example8.1.gm6.

Before we proceed to create our next game, we need to learn a little about something called the DNA, which stands for deoxyribo nucleic acid. If we examine a human cell under a very powerful microscope, we will see a cell structure called the nucleus. Human beings have different kinds of cells that exhibit different behaviors. For example, the cells in the nose have the sense of smell and the cells on the tongue have the sense of taste. Inside a cell, the nucleus has a set of encoded instructions that describe what function the cell should perform. The instructions found inside a molecule are called the DNA. The DNA looks like a twisted ladder and scientists call this structure a double helix. Each of the rungs of the ladder is made up of a combination of two proteins. These proteins are called adenine, thymine, cytosine, and guanine and they have special rules as to how they combine. Adenine can only combine with thymine and cytosine can only combine with guanine.

In this game, you will need to synthesize parts of the DNA. If you can score more than 100 points, you will be considered good at synthesizing the DNA. In the game we are about to play, A represents adenine, T represents thymine, C represents cytosine, and G represents guanine. Thus A pairs with T and C pairs with G according to the rule of genetics. In this game, we have four generators that generate the proteins A, T, C, and G on the top half of the screen. On the bottom half of the screen is a conveyor belt that brings in proteins A, T, C, and G in random order for being paired up. The idea of the game is to pair up the proteins moving along the conveyor belt with appropriate ones created from the generators. Clicking on a generator creates a specific protein. It moves down and if it collides with the right kind of protein, it pairs up and the player is awarded a set of points. Unpaired proteins cause you to lose points. Any score above 50 points, will cause the game to increase in difficulty as proteins move faster along the conveyor belt. When the player exceeds 75 points, the speed increases even more, and reaching a score of 100 points becomes quite challenging.

In short, to play the game you have to click on the correct generator based on the proteins moving on the conveyor belt. If a pair is created, you get points. If a pair is not created, you lose points.

Before we inspect the game objects, let's run the game and play it. The game is easy to start with, but it gets harder as you acquire more points. If you cross 75 points, you may find your score go down quite rapidly, since several proteins on the conveyor belt may leave in an unpaired state. As you test the game out, try to mentally design the objects used. What kind of events do they respond to? What types of actions do they execute? Is there a common behavior that some of them share? This will help you envision the cause and effect relationship of objects in the game.

INSPECTING THE DNA FACTORY GAME

To answer all the questions we just raised and to get a firm understanding of the concept of inheritance, let's inspect the game. Stop the game if you were playing it and look at the resources used to create the game in Game Maker's Resource Explorer. Let's expand on the sprites subfolder. You should see a whole set of sprites, as shown in Figure 8.2.

You may have noticed that the sprites are organized into subfolders called Point-up, Point-down, Generators, and Other. These subfolders allow you to organize your content into subcategories. Creating subfolders is not possible when Game Maker runs in the Standard mode. We need to switch to the Advanced Mode to enable the option to create subfolders. To switch to the Advanced mode, click on the Advanced Mode menu option found under the File menu. If you made any changes to an existing game, you will be prompted to save your changes before the mode is switched. After the mode is switched, you should see the Advanced Mode menu option checked in the file menu.

If you have not yet opened the game file Example8.1.gm6, open it in the Advanced Mode. Expand the Sprites subfolder to see all of the elements shown in Figure 8.2. If you right-click on any of the elements under the Sprites subfolder, you will see a new menu item called Insert Group or Add Group. You can use this option to organize your game resources into subcategories.

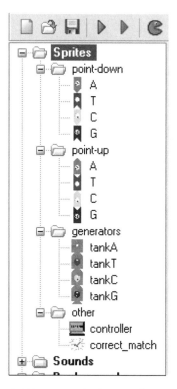

FIGURE 8.2 Sprites used.

In this game, the sprites under the Point-down subcategory are all the sprites used for objects that travel down from the different generator objects. The sprites in the Point-up category include all the sprites that move on the conveyor belt. The sprites under the Generators category are those used on the top half of the screen. The sprites listed under the Other section list all the remaining sprites that did not fit into any of the previous categories.

Now let's inspect the objects used in the game by expanding the Objects subfolder in the Resource Explorer. You should see the objects shown in Figure 8.3.

Four different objects travel down from the generator: A-down, T-down, C-down, and G-down. There are also four other objects that point upward and travel on the conveyor belt: A-up, T-up, C-up, and G-up. All these eight objects are found under the subfolder called Bases in the Resource Tree. In the study of genetics, a *base* refers to one of the four proteins—adenine, thymine, cytosine, and guanine—that is used to create one rung of the DNA double helix. A subfolder called Generators lists all of the objects that create half of the pair required to build one rung of the ladder. There are four generators that create four different types of bases as well as a couple of other objects listed under the Other folder.

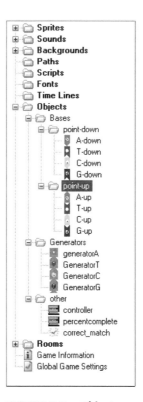

FIGURE 8.3   Objects used.

INSPECTING THE OBJECTS

Now let's look at the different objects and see if it is possible to optimize them. If you open up all the objects under the Point-down subfolder, you will notice that all of them have two events that they respond to: a `Collision` event and an `Outside Room` event. The collision event is different for each of the objects, but the actions they perform are the same. If you look at the actions performed in response to an `Outside Room` event, you will notice they are all the same, so all of the objects in the Point-down folder do the same thing in response to an `Outside Room` event. This particular behavior can be extracted and put inside a parent object. The child object can then inherit this feature from the parent object. Making such a change would move all of the common behaviors to a single point in the parent object. Changes to all of the objects can be implemented by tweaking the parent object's behavior.

INPUTTING THE COMMON BEHAVIOR INTO A PARENT OBJECT

Let's proceed to create a parent object with the common behavior we have isolated among the objects in the Point-down folder. Let's create a new object called `parent-down` in this folder, as shown in Figure 8.4, by right-clicking on the Point-down folder and choosing Add Object.

There is nothing special to be done in creating a parent object. It is just the same as a regular object, so let's add the common event and its associated actions into the parent object. The parent object does not need a sprite since it really does not exist by itself in the game. The child object just inherits properties from the parent object. We'll soon see how that is done.

Let's start adding the common event that we have seen among all the Point-down objects into the `parent-down` object. The event and actions to add to the parent objects are listed in Table 8.1. You may remember that the `Outside Room` event is found in the Other section of the Event Selector pop-up menu.

TABLE 8.1

Event	Action
Outside Room	Destroy instance (self)
	Set score to −1 (relative)

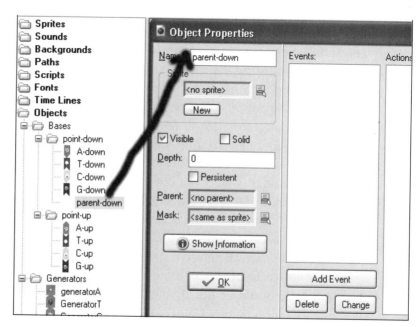

FIGURE 8.4   Creating a parent object.

The completed properties sheet for the parent object is shown in Figure 8.5. After making the changes shown, click the OK button to close the parent object's Property window.

FIGURE 8.5   Parent object for the objects in the Point-down folder.

Now we need to delete the Outside Room event from all the four original objects in the Point-down folder. These are the child objects. Open the A-down object and click on the Outside Room Event to select it. Next, press the Delete button at the bottom of the window to delete the Outside Room event. When prompted for a confirmation, press the Yes button to proceed with the delete operation.

The next change we need to make to the A-down object is to make it a child of the parent-down object. This is done by specifying the parent object in the parent field shown in Figure 8.6. Left-clicking on the text field that says No-parent opens up a pop-up menu that lists the various selections. Navigate to the parent-down object to select it, as shown in Figure 8.6. Congratulations! You have completed the creation of your first parent-child hierarchical relationship.

Next we need to create the other child objects in the Point-down folder. Delete the Outside Room event from the T-down, C-down, and G-down objects. Next set the parent fields to the parent-down object for all these objects just as we did in the previous paragraph for the A-down object. This completes our hierarchical modeling changes for the objects in the Point-down folder. Now play the game and see how it works. There should be no change in behavior, but it is now possible to make changes to the parent object that will automatically be inherited by the child objects. This is a good example of the power of object technology. Small changes in the parent object can be used to unleash changes across a complete hierarchy of objects.

Now let's proceed to inspect the objects in the Point-up subfolder. You may have noticed that all the objects respond to the same events and they also execute the same actions in response to the events. The only difference between the different objects are their names and the sprites attached to them, so it is very easy to extract all the common features and put them into a parent object.

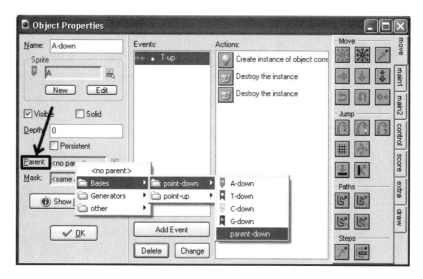

FIGURE 8.6 Choosing the parent object for the objects in the Point-down folder.

Let's start by creating a new object by right-clicking on any object found under the Point-up folder and then choosing the Duplicate menu item from the pop-up menu. This creates a new object with all identical properties. Let's rename this new object parent-up, as shown in Figure 8.7. You may notice that it is populated with all the events and actions available to any of the other objects found in the Point-up subfolder. You may also notice that the parent-up object has a sprite associated with it. Remove the sprite associated with the parent-up object by choosing the No-sprite option as shown highlighted in one of the three boxes in Figure 8.7

We now have our parent object for the Point-up folder ready. We can now delete all of the events and actions for the A-up, T-up, C-up, and G-up objects and assign the parent-up object as the parent for each of them. Figure 8.8 shows the A-up object in the process of being updated with a new parent object, parent-up. You may notice that all of its events have been deleted. You need to repeat the process of assigning a parent object and deleting all the events for the T-up, C-up, and G-up objects.

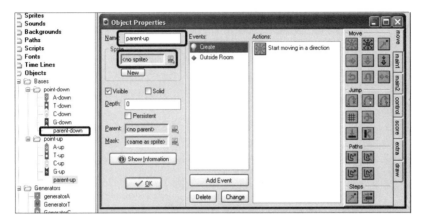

FIGURE 8.7   Parent object for the objects in the Point-up folder.

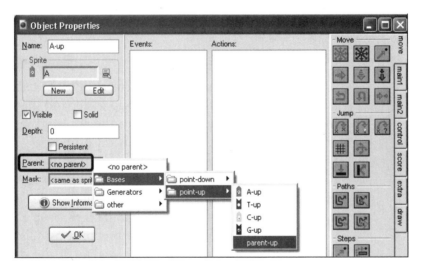

FIGURE 8.8   New child A-up object parented to the parent-up object.

This completes our exercise of creating hierarchical objects. Now you can run the game. Notice how all the objects behave in the same manner. All its child objects will inherit any change made to the parent-up object.

For example, if we want to make the game harder, we can change the speed at which the objects on the conveyor belt move by adjusting the Start Moving in a Direction block used in response to the Create event of the parent-up object. You could now use your knowledge to adjust the speed of the parent object to a lower value to get a higher score.

In this chapter, we looked at using single-level parent-child objects. You could have a complete hierarchy of objects with a grandparent object or great grandparent object if the hierarchy model of the game you create requires it. Now that we have mastered hierarchical objects, let's proceed to the next chapter, where we will be creating a scrolling shooter game.

 The completed example incorporating all the modifications to the DNA game we have created is available in Chapter8\Example8.3.gm6 in the accompanying CD-ROM.

SUMMARY

In this chapter, we looked at the importance of inheritance and learned about the necessity of extracting common behaviors into a parent object. We also switched Game Maker to the advanced mode, looked at the DNA Game, and learned to organize objects hierarchically into folders.

In the DNA Game, we saw how the speed with which the conveyor belt moves depends on the score. The game is initially easy to play. As the score crosses 50 points, things start to move faster. It becomes increasingly difficult to gather points. The game is also run under the control of a timer and it ends at the end of one minute. If the score crosses 75 points, the conveyor belt moves even faster and reaching a score of 100 becomes nearly impossible.

Project

This game could be enhanced to synthesize specific strands of DNA. For example the DNA sequence—ATATCGC-GATCGCGCG—could represent a strand of DNA that needs to be created. Modify the game to enable the player to create this sequence. Reward them appropriately on the completion of the task within certain time limits.

CHAPTER 9

Using Gravity, Paths, Timelines, and Variables

In this chapter:

- Experimenting with Gravity
- Experimenting with Friction
- Using Variables
- Logical Operations
- Paths and Timelines
- Adding Paths
- Using Timelines

In this chapter, we will create games that use some basic concepts of physics. We have used collision, which is one physics concept, extensively in many of the examples in previous chapters. In this chapter, we will use gravitational forces, frictional forces, motion along paths, and timelines. We will create a fruit-picking game where a player needs to pick apples from a tree and avoid being harmed by the insects that fly among the trees. We will also use variables for providing characteristics such as health for individual objects, which are referred to as *bosses* in some games.

EXPERIMENTING WITH GRAVITY

ON THE CD

Now that we are comfortable creating different kinds of objects, let's load up the game Example9.1.gm6 from the Chapter9 directory found on the CD-ROM. This file has two simple prefabricated objects: a ball and a brick. The room consists of a ball placed high above a wall made of bricks. The ball is programmed to bounce off the wall created by a row of bricks once it is set into motion. When we run this game, nothing happens since we have not provided any properties to the ball to set it in motion. Let's change this by adding a gravitational force for the ball object.

To do this, we first need to open the ball object's property sheet by double clicking on `ballObject` in the resource explorer. Let's add a `Create` event by clicking on the Add Event button at the bottom of the Object Properties window. In response to a `Create` event, let's add the `Set Gravity` action as shown in Figure 9.1. The direction field is set to 270 degrees, which makes the gravitational field pull the object to the bottom of the screen. The value for gravity is set to 0.5 pixels per step. The speed of the ball increases by 0.5 pixels per step when the ball moves down and decreases by the same amount when the ball moves up. Let's run the game and see what happens. You should see the ball bouncing indefinitely as though it was in space.

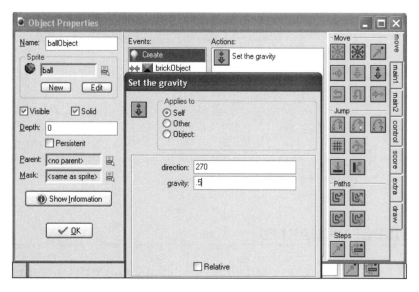

FIGURE 9.1   Setting gravity.

EXPERIMENTING WITH FRICTION

In reality, a ball does not bounce on a surface forever. Let's close the window with the bouncing ball and go back to the ball object's property sheet so that we can add a frictional component. Several kinds of dampening forces can reduce the speed of the object. The most notable among them is friction. In simple terms, friction reduces the speed of an object and dampens its motion. Let's also add a frictional component by adding the Set the Friction action item to the list of actions executed during the Create event, as shown in Figure 9.2. The value to use for this frictional component will be 0.1 pixels per step. Let's run the game and see how the ball behaves. Experiment by changing the values for the friction and gravity and note the ball's behavior. Now let's embark on creating a game that uses gravity and friction along with two more new features: paths and timelines.

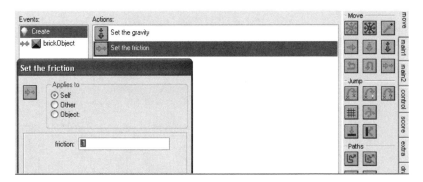

FIGURE 9.2   Setting friction.

USING VARIABLES

Before we use variables, let's learn about what they are and what they can be used for. In simple terms, *variables* are locations where information can be stored. You can think of them as little named cupboards that can be used to save temporary information. This is different from information stored in a hard disk, which is relatively permanent. The lists of actions available for using variables are shown in Figure 9.3.

FIGURE 9.3 Action blocks for variables.

We use variables for storing custom information. For example, Game Maker provides you with a mechanism to keep track of lives and health. This normally refers to the players' lives and health. When the value for health and life become zero, the game ends. We'll call them *global health* and *global lives* since these are more applicable to the game as a whole. Now let's assume we have different enemy objects that need to be shot at one hundred times before they die. This information could ideally be stored in a variable within each enemy object. We can create the variable that serves as a counter when the object is created and assign it a value of our choice, which is one hundred. Every time a bullet hits the enemy object, we can reduce this counter by one. If the counter gets to zero, we can destroy the enemy object.

ON THE CD

Let's look at a simple game that shows you the principle we have described so far. In Game Maker, open the file located in Chapter9\Exercise9.2.gm6 in the CD-ROM. If you expand the Objects subfolder with the Resource Explorer, you will notice that there are five objects. Double-click on the player object with the teddy bear sprite to see the events and actions associated with it. This is the object you control using the cursor keys. Pressing the spacebar makes the teddy bear throw projectiles in the direction in which it is moving. The projectiles are the dot objects that move at a speed of six pixels per step. There are two kinds of enemy objects: the enemy and boss objects. When these two objects collide with the player object, the player loses health. To be specific, when the boss collides with the player, the player loses 50 points of health. When the enemy object collides with the player, the player's health is reduced by 40. If you inspect the actions executed by the enemy and boss objects during a collision event with the player object, you will see the appropriate Set Health action blocks that reduce the health, as shown in Figure 9.4.

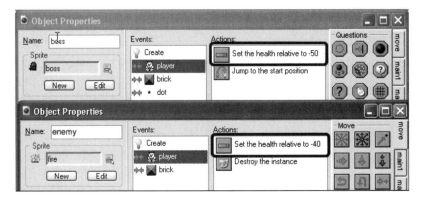

FIGURE 9.4   Action blocks that reduce health.

Now let's play the game for a few minutes before we proceed further and find out how we have used variables to provide health for the boss object. Remember that the cursor keys control the bear and the spacebar is used to shoot. Getting rid of the enemy objects is easy. They are destroyed with one shot, but the boss object needs to be hit ten times.

Now let's open the properties sheet for the boss object to see the actions associated with the Create event. The boss health is already set for you in the following way. The events of interest are the Create event and the Collision event with the dot object. Figure 9.5 shows the Set Variable action in use during the Create event. The Properties box for this action requires you to provide a user-defined name for the variable, which could be anything. It is a good idea to give the variables meaningful names to avoid confusion when you have numerous variables in a more complex game. We have named the variable bosshealth and assigned it an initial value of 100. The important thing to remember is that this variable is applicable only to this instance of the boss. If we create another instance of the boss, that instance would have its own bosshealth variable. The variables that apply to only one instance of the object are appropriately called instance variables in object technology.

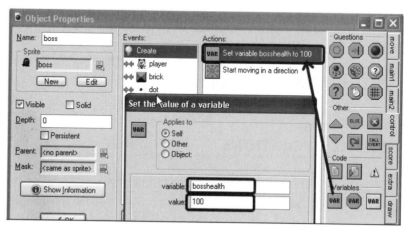

FIGURE 9.5   Setting boss health.

Now let's look at the various actions executed during a Collision event with the dot object. The properties sheet for the action that decrements the value stored inside the bosshealth variable is shown in Figure 9.6.

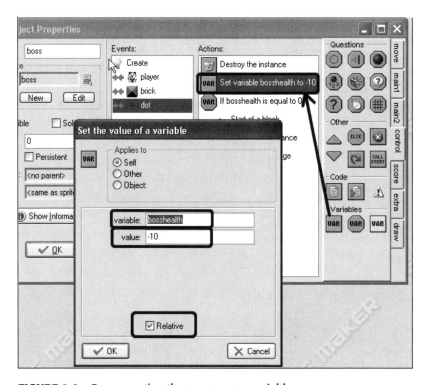

FIGURE 9.6 Decrementing the bosshealth variable.

LOGICAL OPERATIONS

Once the value of the bosshealth variable is decremented, it is necessary to check if the value is zero. In all programming languages, there is a construct called the if statement for checking the value of variables. In Game Maker, this check is done using the action If the Variable Has a Value, which is octagonal in shape and is shown on the right half of Figure 9.7. In Game Maker, all the octagonal icons are used to simulate an if condition.

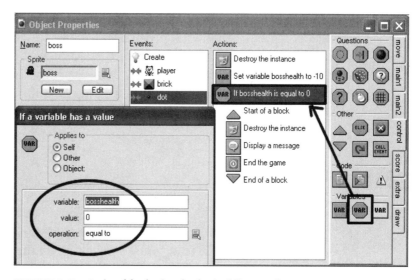

FIGURE 9.7   Action blocks for the logical if operation.

The properties sheet for the action block has been populated with the three entries shown on the lower-left side of Figure 9.7. The action required to check if the bosshealth is equal to zero requires three parameters: the variable (name), the value, and the operation. Another logical operation you could perform with variables is to check if it is greater or less than a predefined value. When you execute a logical operation, you are essentially trying to find out if the operation yields a true or false answer. In our example shown in Figure 9.7, we are trying to find out if the bosshealth is equal to zero. The possible answers are either yes or no. If the answer is yes, we can destroy the boss. If the answer is no, the boss remains in the game.

If you have a list of actions to be performed when a condition is true, you need to put this list of actions inside a start block and an end block. Both of these blocks are triangular and are found in the Control tab. We are executing three actions if the bosshealth is zero. The first one will destroy the boss (destroy self), the next one will display the message "You win!", and the third will end the game.

It is good programming practice to use start and end blocks at all times when working with if statements. If you do not use the start and end blocks, only the first action block will be executed if the condition is true. We will look at this problem in Chapter 10, which deals more specifically with some common troubleshooting problems related to software bugs.

PATHS AND TIMELINES

To use paths and timelines, we need to run Game Maker in the Advanced Mode. If you are not already in the Advanced Mode, change to the Advanced Mode by clicking on the Advanced Mode button in the File Menu.

ON THE CD
Before we delve into paths and timelines, let's close our current file and open a new one using Game Maker. Let's load a new game \Chapter9\Exercise9.3.gm6, located on the CD-ROM. This example provides all the rudimentary pieces we need for building the Pick the Fruit Game. In this game, we have to move the player up a tree using the cursor keys and move it to pick up (collide with) the apple at the top. There are many kinds of insects that start out static. Later, we'll be attaching paths and timelines to the objects to make their movements hard to predict.

Open the Resource Explorer and look at the events and actions of the player object in the player folder. The first action under the Create event for the player is the Set the Gravity action. The player has a gravity action attached to it, so it may be a little hard at first to move it. If the player is moved off the ground using the up arrow, you should be able to move left and right. If you want to go higher, you need to repeatedly press the up arrow to overcome gravity. Let's now play the game by pressing Game Maker Run menu item. Try to move the player toward the apple. Continue until you win this preliminary version of the game. If it is hard, try to reduce the gravity assigned to the player or just go the appropriate room and remove a few objects that are obstacles.

ADDING PATHS

Paths are game resources that can be attached to objects to define a particular path they move along. In a car racing game, for example, you could have several cars moving along an elliptical racecourse with varying speeds.

Let's continue to work with the file we have currently loaded in Game Maker (Example9.3.gm6) and create paths that some of the objects could move along.

Paths are created by right-clicking on the Paths subfolder in the Resource Explorer and choosing the Add Path menu item from the pop-up window. Let's right-click on the Paths subfolder in the Resource Explorer to add a path. You should see the Path Properties box appear with an empty grid on the right. Let's first rename this path `tickpath` as shown in the upper-left corner of Figure 9.8. Tickpath signifies the usage of this path as the one traversed by tick objects. To create a path, left-click on a few locations sequentially inside the grid on the right using Figure 9.8 as a rough guideline. In the Figure, we have clicked on eight locations. The line joining all the points defines a jagged path. To get a smooth path, click

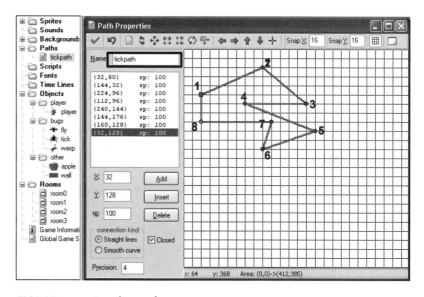

FIGURE 9.8 Creating paths.

on the Smooth Curve radio button on the lower-left corner of the Properties box. After smoothing out the curve, you can click and drag the little blue circles on the right to fine-tune the path. We can now close this Path Properties box and proceed to create a `flypath` and a `wasppath` in just the same way. An example of these paths can be found on the CD-ROM in the location \Chapter9\Exercise9.4.gm6.

The next step is to attach these paths to the objects. Open the properties sheet for the `tick` object and add a `Create` event. Drag the `Set a Path for the Instance` action into the active Actions Area as shown in Figure 9.9. You will see the Properties box for this action. Proceed to set the Path, Speed and At End fields to the values shown in Figure 9.9. Run the game, play it, and come back when you want to proceed to the next step. You will notice that the objects move along the paths you created for them.

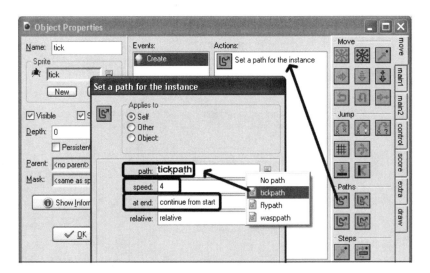

FIGURE 9.9   Set Path Action Properties block.

You should have seen the ticks moving along the path we created. We'll use the Set Path actions block for the `fly` object and the `wasp` object. Assign the `flypath` to the fly and the `wasppath` to the wasp. In the Set Path properties box, set the speed for the fly to be six pixels per step, and ten pixels per step for the wasp. The example provided in CDImage\Chapter9\Exercise9.5.gm6 incorporates all the changes described here. Before you run the game, be prepared to make changes to the room and delete a few objects to make the game a little easier to play. Now run the game—preferably your version. Play it and we'll proceed to the next step.

USING TIMELINES

Timelines are used when you want an object to do different tasks at different times. Use your imagination to think of different ways to use timelines. In our example, we will create a timeline that makes the apple move up and down. We will add two actions to a timeline that are to be done at two different moments of time. We'll continue to use the example we are working with and start creating a timeline. To create a new timeline, click on the Timeline folder in the Resource Explorer and choose the Add Time Line option. You should see the Timeline Properties box appear on the right. Change the name to Updown in the Name field on the upper-left of the Properties box, as shown in Figure 9.10 and click on the Add button to start creating the timeline. In the Add a Moment dialog box that appears, leave the default value at zero and press OK. A value of zero signifies the first step of the timeline. In the Actions section on the right, click and drag the Move Action, as shown in Figure 9.11. Set the speed to four and click on the down arrow so that the object to which this time line is attached will move down too.

Click on the Add button in the Timeline Properties window to add the second item to the list. In the Add a Moment dialog box that pops up, type in a value of 30. One second is equal to about 30 steps. Click OK to close the Add a Moment box. Next, add a Move Action box just as we did earlier, as shown in Figure 9.11. The Up Arrow should be selected in the Move Properties box, and the speed should be set to four pixels per step.

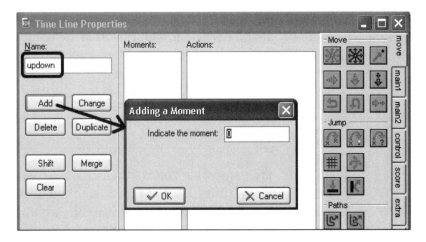

FIGURE 9.10 Timeline properties.

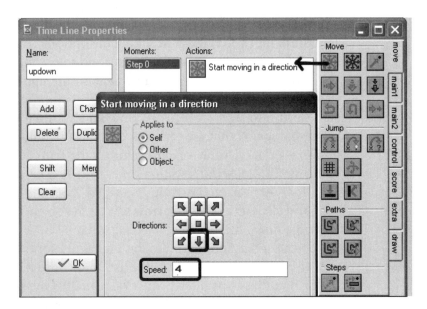

FIGURE 9.11 Adding an action.

Now click on the Add button in the Timeline Properties window to add the third item to the list. In the Add a Moment dialog box that pops up, type in a value of 59. Close this box and add the Set Timeline Position action from the Main2 tab as shown in Figure 9.12. This action makes the object using this timeline reset itself to step 0 after reaching Step 59. You will understand what that means after you attach this timeline to an object and see it working.

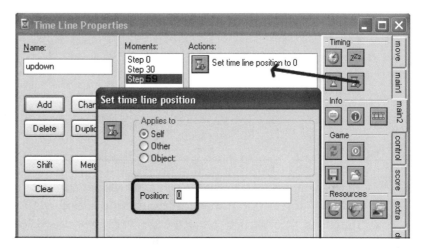

FIGURE 9.12   Setting Timeline Position Properties.

Close the Timeline Properties window and open the Properties window for the apple object. Add a Create event and attach a Set Time Line action to the apple object, as shown in Figure 9.13.

ON THE CD   The example provided in on the CD-ROM has the Game Maker file Chapter9\Exercise9.6.gm6, which incorporates of all the changes described up to this point. Now run the game (preferably your version), play it, and come back when you want to proceed to Chapter 10.

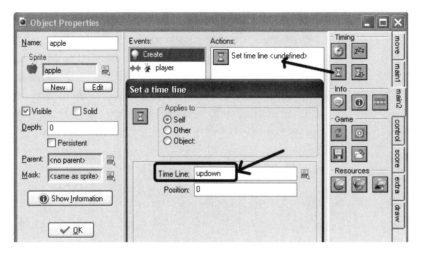

FIGURE 9.13 Setting Timeline Properties.

SUMMARY

In this chapter, we learned to use actions that simulate gravitational forces, frictional forces, motion along paths and timelines. We learned to use the Set Gravity action block to accelerate an object in a specific direction, and we learned to do the opposite and slow down an object by using the Set the Friction action. We also looked at using a variable to describe the health of individual objects.

In addition the use of paths and timelines ws covered, and we learned that paths allow an object to move along a specified curve, timelines enable an object to execute different actions at different points of time.

Project

Make a car racing game using your knowledge of paths. Let a set of cars move along a path that defines the racetrack, and have the player's car be controlled by a set of keys on the keyboard. Include a key for acceleration and one for deceleration. If the player collides against a wall, the player's car will be damaged. This can be reflected by reducing the health of the player. When the health reaches zero, the player looses one life. After the player looses all lives the game ends. The game would also end if the other cars finish the race before the player, and you can add informational messages at appropriate junctures to either warn or reward the player.

CHAPTER 10

Debugging Common Problems

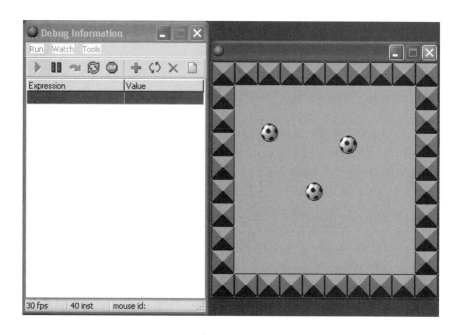

In this chapter:

- Case 1: Unable to Move to a New Level
- Case 2: Invisible Objects Placed Outside the Game Room
- Case 3: Boss Object Is Never Destroyed
- Executing Step by Step
- Using Debug Messages
- If-Then-Else Idiosyncrasies
- Cheat Codes

We have looked at various ways to create different types of games with Game Maker. When you start making games that are based on your own ideas and start creating games from scratch, you most likely will find out that something does not work the way it was intended to. It is very rare in the software world to see projects work flawlessly the first time. There are many kinds of software bugs that may need to be straightened out. A testing and quality assurance department would write a complete test plan to test a final game to its limits in an effort to make sure the final game is as bug-free as possible.

As a game developer, you may spend as much time testing the game as you did building it. If things do not work the way they were supposed to, Game Maker provides a debugging tool that can be used to investigate the cause of the problem. In this chapter, we will look at a couple of simple games that do not work. We will use Game Maker's built-in debugger to investigate the cause of the error.

CASE 1: UNABLE TO MOVE TO A NEW LEVEL

ON THE CD

Let's open the file Chapter10\Example10.1.gm6 in the accompanying CD-ROM. If you inspect the resources, you will see two objects and two rooms. In this game, you have to click on the soccer balls to make them disappear. After all of the soccer balls vanish from the first room, you should go to the next room. Let's play the game for a few minutes and check to see if it is functioning correctly. Then we'll resume our debugging journey.

We don't see the second room, even after we make all of the soccer balls disappear. The first thing we want to do is to check the properties of the ball object by double left-clicking on the ballObject in the Resource Explorer. You could maximize this window to see the actions clearly. There is just one mouse click event that the ball responds to. When the player clicks on the ball object, it does the following actions:

■ Augments the score by 10 points.
■ Destroys the ball object.
■ Checks to see if there are no more instances of the ball object.
■ If there are no more, it goes to the next room.

From this set of actions, it is obvious that we should move to the next room after all the `ballObjects` disappear, but it does not happen. Why?

Let's try to run the game in the debug mode and see if we can find the problem. To run the game in the debug mode, we need to press the Red Arrow button on the Main toolbar (see Figure 2.4 in Chapter 2). You can also press F6 to run the program in the debug mode or click on the Run menu item on the main drop-down menu bar (Figure 2.4) and then choose Run in Debug Mode. When you run the game in the debug mode, you should see the Debug Information window shown in Figure 10.1 along with the regular game window.

Before we play the game, let's open one of the debug windows that lists all the instances running in the game by clicking on the Show Instances menu selection under the Tools menu, as shown in Figure 10.2.

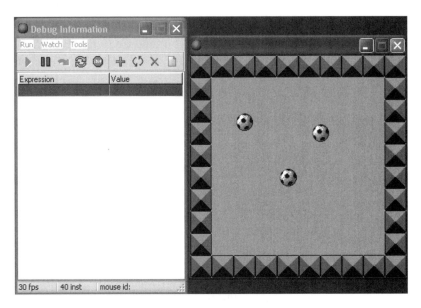

FIGURE 10.1   The Debug Information window.

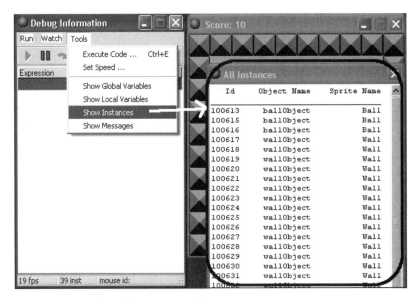

FIGURE 10.2   The All Instances window.

The All Instances window lists all the instances of objects you have used in your game. In this window, you can see the identification number (ID) of the instance, the name of the object, and the name of the sprite that it uses.

With this window open, let's play the game. The game will run a little slower than usual since it is running concurrently with the debugger. You may notice that the number of ballObjects listed in the All Instances window reduces in number as you click on the ballObjects in the game window. When all the ballObjects disappear in the game window, we still have one left in the All Instances window. We cannot see this instance on the screen, but the debugger tells us that there is one object lurking somewhere. Since Game Maker knows that there is one instance hidden in some obscure corner, it does not allow you to the next room.

From the current status of the All Instances window, we know that the ID of the mystery ballObject is 100613. We'll get more information about object 100613 by looking at the object's local variables. From the Debug Information window, click on Tools > Show Local Variables. You should see the dialog box shown in Figure 10.3. Let's enter the mystery ballObject's ID into this window and click the OK button.

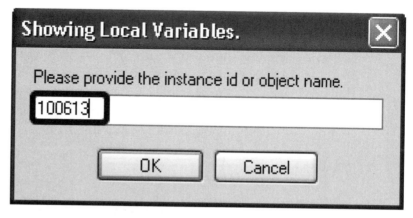

FIGURE 10.3   Object ID dialog box.

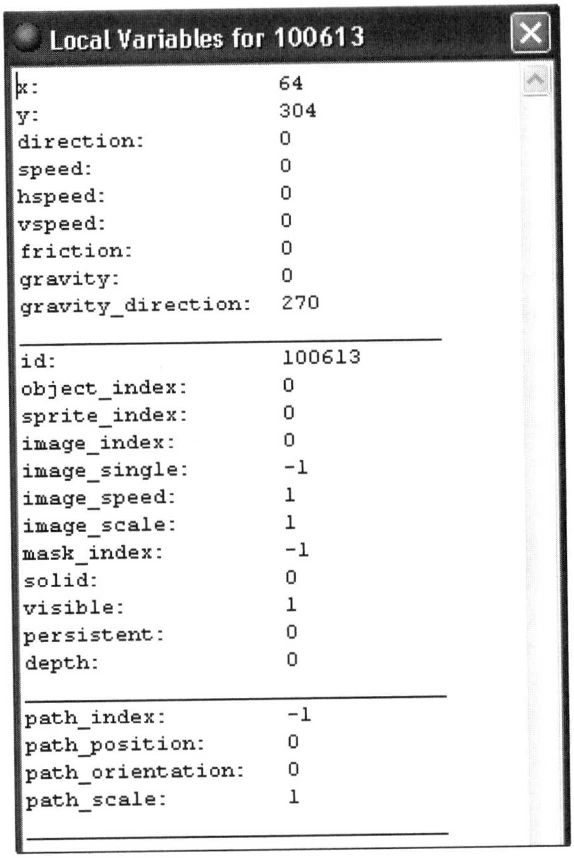

FIGURE 10.4 Local Variables window.

A new window should open up that lists all the object's local variables, as shown in Figure 10.4. The first two lines of this window give us the valuable clue as to where this object is. The mystery `ballObject` has its X coordinate set to 64 and its Y coordinate set to 304, as shown in Table 10.1.

TABLE 10.1

X Coordinate	Y Coordinate
64	304

Note this number on a sheet of paper. Then go back and inspect the room to see if you can find it. Close game and return to the Resource Explorer and open the properties of room1 found under the Rooms subfolder. If you move your cursor inside the Room Properties window, you should see the current coordinates of the cursor at the bottom of the window, as shown in Figure 10.5.

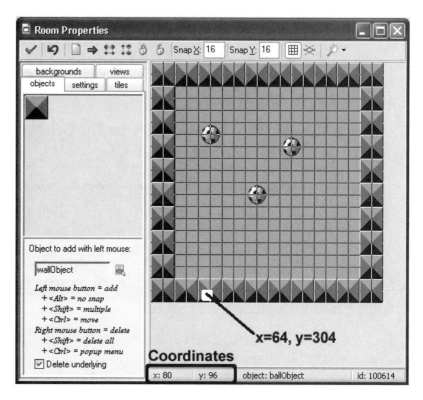

FIGURE 10.5   Coordinates for the object.

Now let's locate the coordinates where X is 64 and Y is 304. This is where the mystery ballobject is, but we do not see it. If you right-click on the top half of the brick at this location to remove the brick, you will see the hidden ballObject (Figure 10.6) underneath the BrickObject that has been causing us grief.

You can remove this ballObject from the room, replace the removed bricks, and then play the game. Everything should function normally.

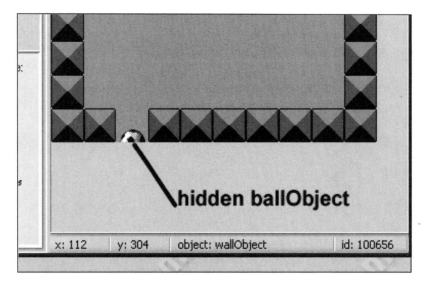

x: 112 | y: 304 | object: wallObject | id: 100656

FIGURE 10.6 Coordinates for the object.

CASE 2: INVISIBLE OBJECTS PLACED OUTSIDE THE GAME ROOM

ON THE CD
The problem described here is very similar to Case 1. Let's open the file Chapter10\Example10.2.gm6 and play the game for a few minutes. You will notice again that you are not taken to the second room even after you destroy all the ballObjects. Just like the earlier problem, there is a mystery ball hidden somewhere. Since these balls start moving as soon as they are created, we don't have a way to find out where they started. The best way would be to set the speed to zero in the ballObject's Create event, as shown in Figure 10.7 so that they do not move. We can then find out if there are any hidden ballObjects tucked away anywhere else.

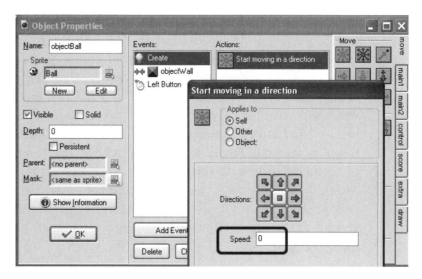

FIGURE 10.7   Resetting speed to zero.

If you press F6 to run the game in the debug mode and follow the same procedure we used for Case 1, you will find that two `ballObjects` are outside the room, with IDs 100653 and 100654.

The object with ID 100653 can be found at the location where X is 144 and Y is 384 (Figure 10.8). The object with ID 100654 can be found at the location where X is 496 and Y is 224 (Figure 10.8). If you place your mouse at the bottom righthand corner of the room, you will see that the maximum value for the X and Y coordinate inside the room is 288. One or more of the coordinates of both the objects we are investigating are greater than the room size, so these objects are outside the room.

Local Variables for 100653		Local Variables for 100654	
x:	144	x:	496
y:	384	y:	224
direction:	270	direction:	270
speed:	0	speed:	0
hspeed:	0	hspeed:	0
vspeed:	0	vspeed:	0
friction:	0	friction:	0

FIGURE 10.8   Local variables.

The easiest way to get rid of them is to place another object outside the room. This is done by left-clicking inside the room and then dragging the mouse outside the room. This would place an object outside the room. If you click on the green check mark on the top-left corner of the Room Properties window to save the room, you will be prompted with a dialog box that informs you that there are objects outside the room, as shown in Figure 10.9. Click on the Yes button to remove the offending objects and this will solve the problem. After that you can reset the speed of the `ballObject` during its `Create` event back to four pixels per step to get a working version of the game. Now you can play the game and go to the winning screen.

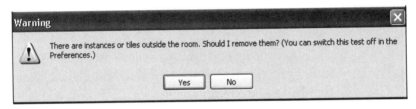

FIGURE 10.9   Deleting objects outside room.

CASE 3: BOSS OBJECT IS NEVER DESTROYED

ON THE CD

Now let's look at a game in which we have an enemy object, called a `bossObject` in some games, that does not die. Let's open the file Chapter10\Example10.3.gm6. If you inspect the resources used in this game, you will see five objects and one room. This game is a buggy version of the game we created in earlier chapters. The player controls the teddy bear. You have to get rid of all the fire and the boss by shooting dots on them. Pressing the spacebar shoots the dots. Fire is destroyed when a single dot strikes it. The boss object looses 15 points of health for every shot that hits it. Figure 10.10 shows you the actions executed when a dot strikes the boss. When the boss's health runs down to zero, the object is destroyed and you win the game.

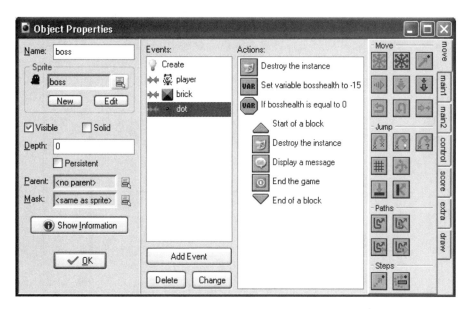

FIGURE 10.10 Boss object properties.

Now let's play the game. However hard you try, you will not be able to win the game because the boss object will never die. To see where the problem is, let's rerun the game in the debug mode. Open the Local Variables window for the boss object using the ID of 100082, as shown in Figure 10.11. You will notice that the last row of this window shows the value of the variable called `bosshealth`. It should start at 100 and reduce every time a dot hits the boss. Strike the boss several times to see what happens to this value. You'll notice that it becomes negative after some time. The game was supposed to end when the `bosshealth` variable reached a value of zero, but that never happened.

It's time to go back and take another look at the properties shown in Figure 10.10. Open the Properties window for the boss object and select the collision with the dot event.

You may notice that the fourth action checks to see if the value of the bosshealth variable is equal to zero. This condition never happens since we are deducting 15 points for every collision of the dot object with the boss object. Starting with a health of 100, the bosshealth will reduce gradually to 85, 70, 55, 40, 25, 10, −5, −20, and so on. It never becomes equal to zero, so the boss object never gets destroyed.

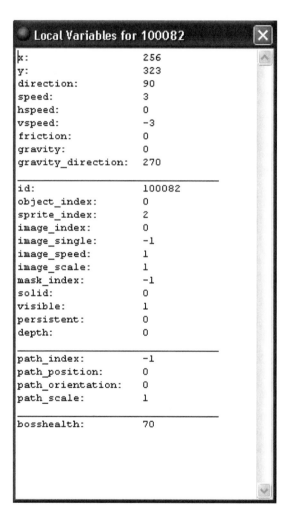

Local Variables for 100082	
x:	256
y:	323
direction:	90
speed:	3
hspeed:	0
vspeed:	-3
friction:	0
gravity:	0
gravity_direction:	270
id:	100082
object_index:	0
sprite_index:	2
image_index:	0
image_single:	-1
image_speed:	1
image_scale:	1
mask_index:	-1
solid:	0
visible:	1
persistent:	0
depth:	0
path_index:	-1
path_position:	0
path_orientation:	0
path_scale:	1
bosshealth:	70

FIGURE 10.11   Local variables for the boss object before bosshealth becomes negative.

To fix this problem, let's change the fourth action box to check if the `bosshealth` is less than zero rather than equal to zero, as shown in Figure 10.12. If seven dots hit the boss, the boss's health will become less than zero. The boss will get destroyed and you will win the game.

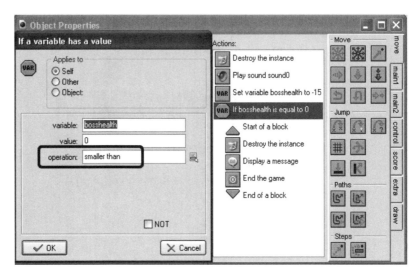

FIGURE 10.12   Smaller than zero check.

EXECUTING STEP BY STEP

The Game Maker engine works by doing different tasks in small, predefined slices of time. A second of time is split up into 30 tiny slices by default. Each slot of time corresponds to one-thirtieth of a second and is called a *step*. In the debug mode, we can see how objects behave at every step.

ON THE CD   Open the game in Chapter10\Example10.4.gm6 and run it in the debug mode. In the Debug Information window, press the Pause button shown in Figure 10.13. Now you can click on the Single Step button to see the game progress one step at a time. You'll see all the objects move the amount they are supposed to for every step. The fire objects, for example, will move four pixels every time you press the Single Step button.

There are many other things that you could learn from the Debug Information window. Clicking on Tools > Global Variables will give you information about the health, score, mouse position, and more. You could use the Watch > Add to display a variable you'd like to track. The speed of an object can be determined by looking at the object's Local Variables property window (Figure 10.4).

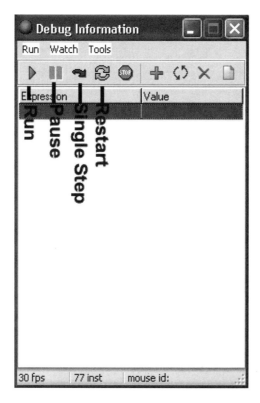

FIGURE 10.13   Debug Information window.

USING DEBUG MESSAGES

Debug messages are small text messages you can display in a special window when the game is running in the debug mode. To generate debug messages, you need to execute a function called `show_debug_message ()`. Open the game in Chapter10\Example10.4.gm6 once again, and we will modify it to print out a message every time the boss bounces against a wall.

To use debug messages, we need to make small changes to the boss object and incorporate calls to the `show_debug_message` function. Open the properties box for the boss object and see what happens during a `Collision` event with the wall object. There should be just one action associated with this event that makes the boss bounce. Next add the `Execute a Piece of Code` action block from the Control tab, as shown in Figure 10.14.

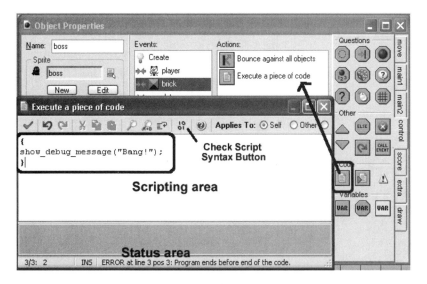

FIGURE 10.14   Execute a piece of code.

You should see the Execute a Piece of Code window appear. We need to type the following script into the scripting area shown in Figure 10.14. Do not leave out any characters or symbols.

```
{
show_debug_message("Bang!");
}
```

We can check to see if the syntax is right by pressing the Check Script Syntax button shown in Figure 10.14. Error messages will appear in the status area at the bottom of the same window. We can now close this scripting window by clicking on the green check mark at the top left corner of this window.

Now we are ready to test this change in the debug mode. Run the game in the debug mode and then click on Tools > Show Messages. A new Messages window (Figure 10.15) should appear, and every time the boss object hits the wall, you should see a Bang! message pop-up in this window.

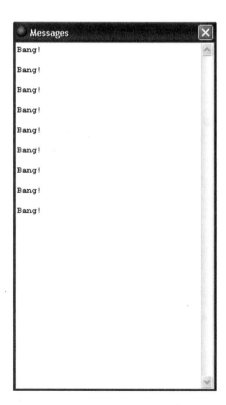

FIGURE 10.15   Messages window.

IF-THEN-ELSE IDIOSYNCRASIES

ON THE CD

To illustrate problems that can arise because of incorrectly formatted if-then-else conditional statements, let's load up the file Chapter10\Example10.4.gm6.

Run the game. You'll notice that as soon as you hit the boss with one dot, you win the game. The boss was supposed to take at least seven hits before dying. Let's open the properties for the boss object (Figure 10.16).

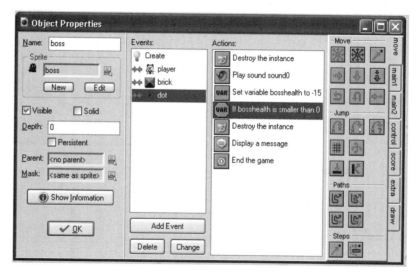

FIGURE 10.16 Boss Properties window.

You'll notice that the fourth action on the right checks to see if the `bosshealth` variable is smaller than zero. We expect the next three blocks to execute only if the `bosshealth` is smaller than zero, but that will not happen. The `Display Message` and `End Game` actions will always be executed, but the `Destroy` action beneath the If Bosshealth Is Smaller Than Zero will be executed only when the `bosshealth` is smaller than zero.

To correct this problem, you need to use Start Of A Block and End Of A Block actions to keep all the actions that need to be executed together, as shown in Figure 10.17.

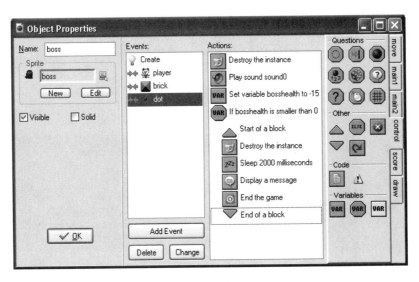

FIGURE 10.17 Using start and end blocks.

CHEAT CODES

Cheat codes enable game designers to skip levels during functional tests of the game. As the complexity in game levels increase, it becomes challenging to complete each level before proceeding to the next level of the game. At some point, the challenge may prevent the game creator from reaching the final levels of the game. Fixing any problems that might be present at those levels becomes cumbersome. Cheat codes permit you to skip levels and add extra lives, health, bonuses, and more.

ON THE CD
Open the game located on the CD-ROM Chapter10\ Example10.5.gm6. Play the game. You may notice that it is increasingly challenging to complete each level. If we want to test the third level of the game, we'd like a quick way of

getting there. To do this, we will have to create a cheat code to allow us to skip levels.

To begin, close the game. In the Resource Explorer, add a new object by right-clicking on the group labeled Other inside the Objects folder. We are placing this object in the Other folder because it doesn't belong to the categories of player or bugs. Let's name this object tweak. Because we do not need to see the object, we are going to uncheck the Visible option. Now we need to decide what keyboard key is going to be our cheat code. Next click the Add Event button in the Object Properties window. Click on the event Keyboard and select the letter T from the keypad, as shown in Figure 10.18. This means the letter T will be our cheat code. Whenever the game player presses T during the game, the game will skip a level.

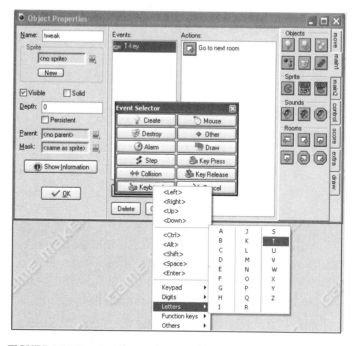

FIGURE 10.18　Creating a cheat code.

Next select the Main1 tab in the Actions browser and click on the Go to Next Room icon, as shown in Figure 10.19.

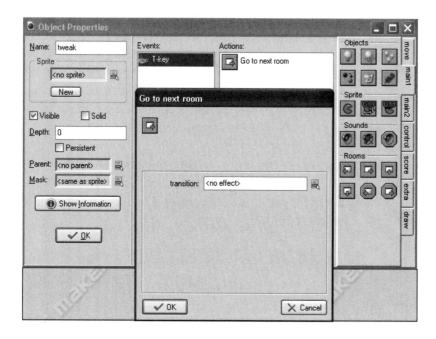

FIGURE 10.19   Control Action for cheat code.

Keep the default values. Click OK to close the Go to Next Room Action. Click OK to close the Object Properties window. Place the object tweak in each room of the game, as shown in Figure 10.20. Run the game and try pressing the T key on the keyboard. The game should skip to the next level, allowing you to debug the game if necessary.

The example game (Chapter10\Example10.6.gm6) provided on the CD-ROM has a completed version with a cheat code. Test it and see if you can skip levels with the cheat code used in this game. Create a game executable and check if your friends can figure out the the cheat code.

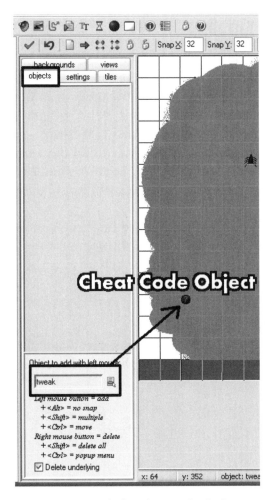

FIGURE 10.20 Placing cheat codes in the Game room.

SUMMARY

In this chapter we looked at ways to solve problems when things do not work. We used the Game Maker Debug tool to inspect instances and their properties, while a game is running. Using the properties window of an instance, we can accurately pin point its position, its speed of motion, and the state of its other internal variables. Remember that the object properties window is very useful for debug situations when things do not happen when a certain condition is met. It is also possible to execute the game step-by-step in a very slow fashion to understand how the engine functions on every game cycle.

In addition, we learned that if-then-else idiosyncrasies typically cause a lot of problems for those using logical blocks for the first time, the Start of Block and End of Block actions prove very useful to take care of most bugs that arise in such situations.

We also looked at the implementation of cheat codes. These are useful during the game-testing phase when it is necessary to take a shortcut to move to a specific room within the game.

Project

As an exercise, try adding a cheat code for the DNA game that slows it down when the game becomes too hard to play.

CHAPTER 11

Finishing Touches

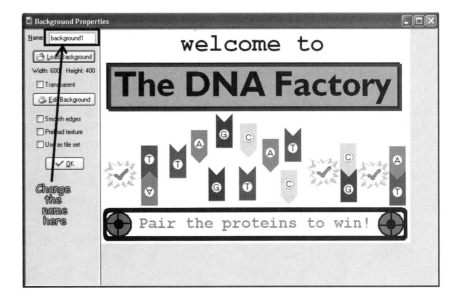

In this chapter:

- Creating the Title Page
- Background Music
- Game Playing Instructions
- Publishing and Distributing the Game
- Conclusion

CREATING THE TITLE PAGE

The title page for the game is the first screen that a player sees when the game is loaded. It is a good idea to create a title page with graphics that portray an image that summarizes some of the key elements of the game. For example, you could have all the sprites nicely arranged on a suitable background. In Game Maker, the title page is the first room the player visits. Usually there is just one object in this room that plays the role of a start button. When this object either receives a Mouse Click event or a specific keyboard event, the Go To Next Room action is executed.

Title pages can be created using a graphics editor of your choice. It is a good idea to restrict the size of the title page to be equal to that of the room. Game Maker allows the use of external images in several different file formats such as jpeg, bmp, tiff, and more.

Let's load the DNA Factory game from Chapter11/Example11.1.gm6 on the CD-ROM and add a title screen to it. If you expand the resources found in the Rooms folder, you should see one room called room1 and one background called Conveyor in the Backgrounds folder, as shown in Figure 11.1.

Now let's add a ready-made background that will be used for our title page. Right-click on the Backgrounds subfolder in the Resource Explorer shown in Figure 11.1, and choose Add Background. You should see the Backgrounds Property window, as shown in Figure 11.2. Click on the Load Background button and you should be prompted with a file selection window.

dow. On the CD-ROM, image files that can be used for the

background are found in the Resources/Backgrounds directory, as shown in Figure 11.3. Choose the file DNATitle.bmp and load it.

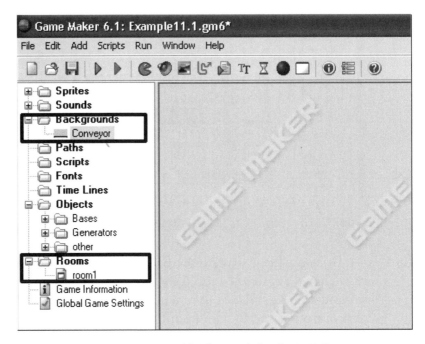

FIGURE 11.1   Rooms and backgrounds for the DNA Factory game.

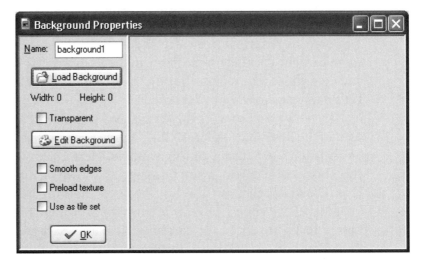

FIGURE 11.2   Background properties.

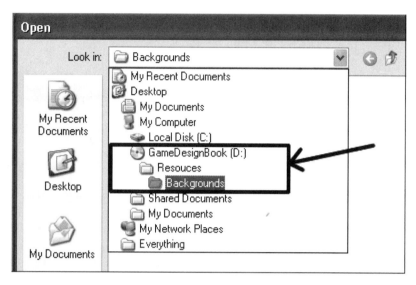

FIGURE 11.3 Location of files on CD-ROM.

Once the file is loaded, the Background Properties window changes and you should be able to see the new background. It is a good idea to rename this background with an appropriate name to avoid confusion when you have numerous files. Type "DNATitle" into the textbox shown in Figure 11.4 and close that window. Next we need to create a new room. Right-click on the Rooms folder in the Resource Explorer and select Add Room. A new room is created in the Resource Explorer, as shown in Figure 11.5. Rename this room by right-clicking on the name in the Resource Explorer and then choose the rename button, as shown in Figure 11.5. Let's name this new room TitleRoom.

Open the properties for the TitleRoom by double-clicking on it in the Resource Explorer. Click on the Backgrounds tab on the upper-left corner of this window. Next click on the checkbox marked Foreground Image, as shown in Figure 11.6. Let's also click on the box beneath the Foreground Image label and choose DNATitle from the pop-up menu, as shown in Figure 11.6. We can now close the Background Properties box by clicking on the green checkmark at the top left corner.

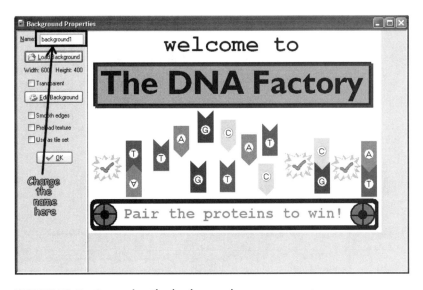

FIGURE 11.4 Renaming the background. Images courtesy of Ramya Swamy. Reprinted with permmission.

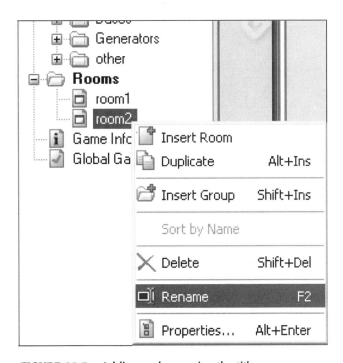

FIGURE 11.5 Adding and renaming the title room.

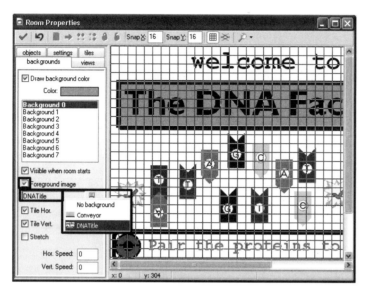

FIGURE 11.6 Placing the foreground image. Images courtesy of Ramya Swamy. Reprinted with permmission.

In the Rooms folder, the rooms are displayed in the order in which they are loaded. In the example we are working on, room1 is our first room and the TitleRoom is the next one. We need TitleRoom to be the first room and room1 to be the next one. Clicking and dragging the rooms found in the Resource folder changes their loading order. Since we want the title room to be our first room to load, let's click and drag Title-Room over room1, as shown in Figure 11.7. TitleRoom becomes the first room to load. Let's rename room1 GameRoom so that we clearly understand what each of the two rooms are used for.

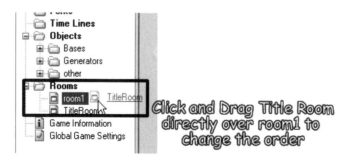

FIGURE 11.7 Changing the room loading order.

With our rooms in place, we need to next create an object that will transition the game from the title room to the game room. Create a new object by right-clicking on the subfolder named Other within the Objects subfolder in the Resource Explorer, as shown in Figure 11.8. Name this object start by typing in this name inside the textbox shown in Figure 11.8.

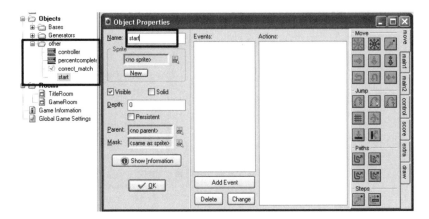

FIGURE 11.8 New start object.

Now we are going to add a global mouse event to this object by clicking on the Add Event button. Let's select the Mouse event, followed by the Global Mouse event, and finally the Global Left Button, as shown in Figure 11.9.

The last thing we need to do to complete the start object is to add an action to it. The action that will take us to the next room is found under the Main1 tab, as shown in Figure 11.10. Drag and drop that into the Actions Area, as shown in Figure 11.10. You can then close the start object's property box.

Now that we have a start object ready, we need to place it inside the TitleRoom. To do this, we need to first open the Title-Room's Property box by double-clicking on it in the Resource Explorer. Choose the Object tab within the TitleRoom's Property box, as shown in Figure 11.11. Next left-click on the Object Selection box shown on the bottom left of the Properties box

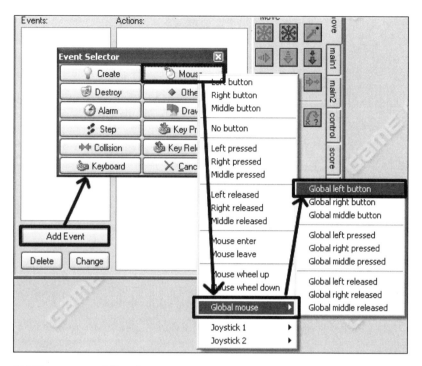

FIGURE 11.9 Adding the Global Mouse event.

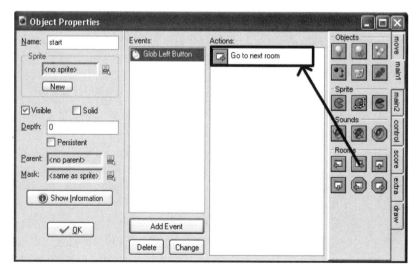

FIGURE 11.10 Completing the start object.

and then navigate through the pop-up menu boxes to choose the start object, as shown in Figure 11.11.

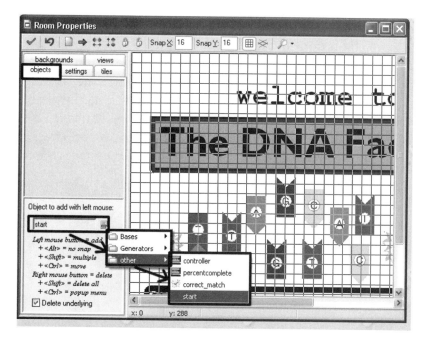

FIGURE 11.11 Placing the start object in the room. Images courtesy of Ramya Swamy. Reprinted with permmission.

With this object selected, we can left-click anywhere inside the room (the area with the grid in Figure 11.11) to place an instance of the start object.

You are now ready to play the game. When you press the Run button, you should see the title screen. Clicking anywhere on the title screen takes you to the main game room.

That completes our title screen creation project.

BACKGROUND MUSIC

To have background music play throughout the game, the music file needs to be loaded as a resource into Game Maker. This is done by right-clicking on the Sounds resource folder and then choosing Add Sound. When the sound is used as an action, make sure the loop option is set to True, as shown in Figure 11.12. Since we do not know how long the player will play a game, we cannot use music of a predefined length. We should use a small music clip and play it over and over again if required. Setting the loop option to True makes the music play for as long as the game is running.

FIGURE 11.12 Looping sound.

GAME PLAYING INSTRUCTIONS

Whenever a game is created, a set of instructions go with it. A description of the complete storyline of the game would be beneficial to the player. The game player also needs to know what controls are used in the game. The player would also like to know how points are rewarded and how health and lives are lost. All these details are typed into the Game Information Worksheet. The Game Information sheet can be opened by double-clicking on its icon in the Resource Explorer. A completed Game Information Sheet for the DNA Factory games is shown in Figure 11.13.

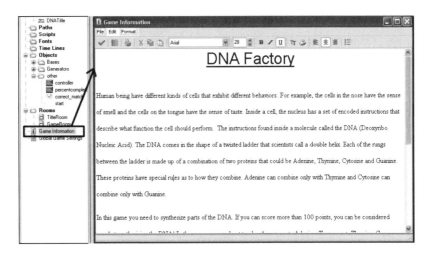

FIGURE 11.13   DNA Factory Game Information Sheet.

The Game Information window is just like any text editor. It allows you to type in any information about the game that you think will be useful to the player. It is also a good idea to have a credits area in the Game Information Worksheet that describes all the team members who played a part in creating the game. For example, maybe one person designed the graphics and another designed the background music. The information that is typed into the Game Information Sheet will be visible when the player presses the F1 key on the keyboard while playing the game.

PUBLISHING AND DISTRIBUTING THE GAME

The final and most interesting part of game design is to make it available to others. Your game could be a business deal where you sell your game to potential buyers or it could be something you provide free of charge. In either case, one needs to provide the game in a format that is easily usable. Thus it does not make sense to send someone the Game Maker files that we have been working with throughout this book. To run the game, they will need Game Maker installed on their machines, which is not practical.

Luckily Game Maker provides us with a mechanism that can create a single executable file that is completely portable across most Microsoft Windows environments. This single executable file contains all of the music, sprites, objects, backgrounds, and other resources, all neatly packaged into one file that can be run independently.

To create this executable file, click on the File menu item and choose Create Executable, as shown in Figure 11.14.

ON THE CD

You will be prompted for the name of the executable file to create. Clicking the Save button creates an independent executable file. This file can be burned onto a CD-ROM and distributed. You could actually sell the games you create and make some money.

FIGURE 11.14 Creating
the final executable file.

FINAL THOUGHTS

Game Design is an amalgamation of several fields including the arts, science, music, and engineering. Artists can create complex digital characters, scientists can design simulation engines that mimic real-world phenomena, musicians can compose the sounds that add extra dimensions to a game, and engineers can perform all of the computations that make the games run. Over the next few years, we are bound to see historians create games that replay important historical events and doctors create game simulations that mimic many surgical procedures. Game Design is for everyone and we sincerely hope that your own game-designing journey flourishes and leads you onto interesting—and perhaps unknown— paths.

SUMMARY

In this chapter we learned to incorporate the title page into a game using mouse and keyboard events and the Go To Next Room action. We looked at the DNA game in depth starting with the first room, we learned to incorporate background music, and how to create a game help screen. We also looked at the mechanism to publish a Game Maker game that can then be distributed on a CD-ROM.

Project

As an exercise, try to make a Mario-style game. Make the game room big enough so that you don't have to scroll the background. Try to use realistic backgrounds. If you do not want to spend time creating the characters, you may be able to find suitable graphics on the web that do not have copyright issues. We'll be exploring platform games extensively in the next chapter.

CHAPTER 12

Platform Games

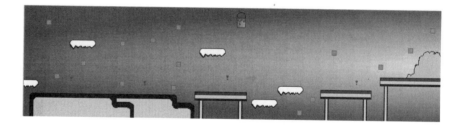

In this chapter:

- Platform Games
- Loading the Game
- Game Room Design
- Components of a Platform Game
- The Player Sprites
- Creating the Rooms
- Designing the Game Objects
- The Color Objects
- The Tutorial Objects
- The Robo Object
- Enemy Objects
- Conclusion

In this chapter, we will look at a couple of different types of games. All of these games are complete games that can be customized to your liking. We will look at a platform game, a scrolling shooter (similar to *Space Invaders*), and then a modified version of *Pacman*.

We will provide you with a working framework that you can enhance and customize to your liking. We will not be building a game from scratch, but will use a working framework and inspect the key components that constitute a platform game. You will then have the ability to create your own. Since creating games without writing scripts and programs is much easier, we will avoid them. We have purposefully avoided using scripts to make the game creation process gentle and easy. It is good to bear in mind, however, that to create more complex games, some level of scripting will need to be incorporated.

PLATFORM GAMES

A typical platform game is one in which the player has to move along or jump across platforms and ledges. There may be enemies along the way that need to be destroyed or objects that need to be collected. *Super Mario Bros.*® from Nintendo® is a typical platform game that has revolutionized the video game industry. Platform games have entertained people for the past 30 years and have evolved significantly.

The platform game we are working on in this chapter is called The Color Game. In this game, the player enters a world in which there is no color. Everything is dull and gray. The player starts with three lives, and the player's goal is to navigate over all the rooms in the game and collect all the color that can be found. Color pigments are placed on different areas of the room. Some of them are easy to pick, while some need a reasonable skill level that one assimilates with extended game play experience. Picking up pigments awards the player one point. Apart from pigments, color is also stored in large paint cans. The player needs to jump against these cans to release the color from within the paint can. The player is awarded five points for each paint can opened. The player's score goes up with every color item that is picked up. There are deep crevices that you can fall through while jumping across platforms in your search for color. Such falls result in the loss of one life. After all the color is picked up, you move to the next level. The game ends when you pick up all the color.

LOADING THE GAME

ON THE CD

Before we start working on understanding how a platform game is made, let us play the version that comes with this book. In Game Maker, open the file Chapter12\Exercise12.1.gm6 on the CD-ROM. Run the Game in the Tutorial mode by Clicking on the Start screen with your Left Mouse button. The only instructions you need to play the game are the use of three keys: the left and right arrow keys for navigating to the left and right, and the Spacebar key for jumping. The tutorial blocks will assist you with all the other information you need.

GAME ROOM DESIGN

The Color Game uses a concept that we have not talked about yet. This concept deals with the use of platforms and the mechanisms used to construct them. Platform games usually consist of a huge room, the dimensions of which far exceed the dimensions of the screen. It is usually difficult to see the complete room in one snapshot. A player typically navigates using a view into the game room. The size of the view is a fixed dimension on the screen but a small portion of the complete room. An object designated as the `Scroller` object moves around under the control of the player inside the view. When this object gets close to the boundaries of the view, the game is scrolled horizontally, vertically, or in both directions to show a new view of the huge game room. The `Scroller` object still remains in the view of the player. To the game player it will seem as though he entered a new area of the game room. The game player vicariously becomes an explorer and discovers the unknown areas of the room beyond what is visible on the screen. The view changes dynamically as the player moves the scroller object around.

We will now look into the design aspects of the construction of the platform itself, and then we will look into the creation of views, scroller objects, enemies, and more.

COMPONENTS OF A PLATFORM GAME

To start building a platform game, one needs to design the basic graphical elements required for building structures.

Not only do these elements need to be reusable building blocks, but they should also be used in the construction of platforms of different kinds. For example, if we want to create a game that has different kinds of platforms like that shown in Figure 12.1, how do we proceed?

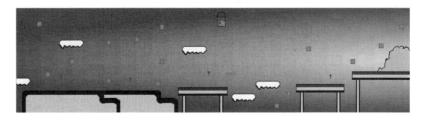

FIGURE 12.1   A typical platform.

When you look at Figure 12.1, it may seem that creating rooms for platform games is quite a complicated process. There seem to be several different kinds of sprites, tables, clouds, and islands in use. The tables and islands are also of different sizes. Things would become easy if the underlying graphical framework was designed such that different basic components can interlock with each other to create more complex components. We will see how it is possible to assemble different kinds of clouds, tables, and islands with just a few well-designed basic graphic components. How would you design the components that could be used to build the element that looks like a table? Could it be a single sprite? You could use a single sprite, but if you wanted to create a slightly longer table, you would need to recreate it since the compoent does not interlock. This would make building a platform a laborious process.

Instead, if we could split the table into three types of components: the left side of the table, the top of the table, and the right side of the table, as shown in Figure 12.2, things would become a little bit easier when we want to create our own custom tables.

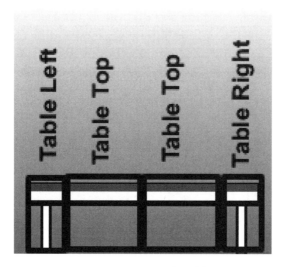

FIGURE 12.2   Components of a table.

If we had the three components saved as three different sprites, we can create tables of all sizes. With one Table Left sprite, one Table Top sprite, and one Table Right sprite, we could create a short table, as shown below in Figure 12.3.

FIGURE 12.3   A short table.

With one Table Left sprite, four Table Top sprites, and one Table Right sprite, we could create a long table, as shown in Figure 12.4.

FIGURE 12.4   A long table.

We now have a design for three sprites that can be used to create tables of any kind. The sprites are shown in Figure 12.5

FIGURE 12.5   Table construction components.

Similar to the sprites used to construct tables, we have created another set of sprites to create islands in our game. These sprites are shown in Figure 12.6. The size of the islands can be customized based on the number of IslandTop sprites we use. You will notice that these sprites also link to one another allowing us to create customized islands of any size.

FIGURE 12.6   Island construction components.

Two other sprites are used for constructing platforms. They are located in the Sprites section of the loaded game and are found in the Platform Components subgroup. They are named Bigblock and Cloud. These two sprites are not interlockable. They can be used independently to create obstacles and paths for the platform game. You could also use other sprites, such as the Bush sprite found in the same section, to bring elements that resemble real-world items into your platform game.

Now let's look at Figure 12.1 again. You may notice that putting together different combinations of sprites creates the platforms. We now have the ability to create all kinds of platforms for our game. You can look at the premade rooms in the game (exercise 12.1.gm6) that you loaded earlier. Let us proceed to the next section, where we will look at the process used to create sprites for the main character of the platform game.

THE PLAYER SPRITES

In The Color Game, the main character is named Robo. We need to create several sprites to represent Robo in different poses. For example, we need a sprite that depicts Robo standing. To make Robo look realistic, we can use an animated gif sequence like the one shown in Figure 12.7. If you view the animated sprite using the sprite editor, you will see the character breathing and moving up and down.

We also need animated sprites to depict our character running to the left and right (Figure 12.8). Once you create an animated sequence for running to the right, you can transform each of the sprites laterally by 180-degrees and create the sequence for running to the left.

We need one sprite for the jumping motion and one for the ducking motion that precedes a jump. Creating these two sprites—named jump and duck—is quite straightforward. Many other sprites are used for other objects, as shown in Figure 12.9

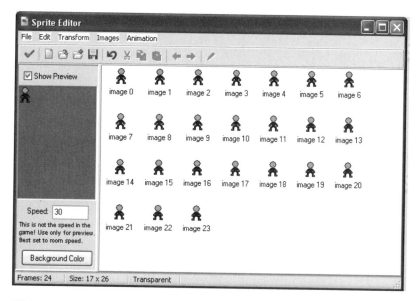

FIGURE 12.7   Animated gif sequence showing Robo standing.

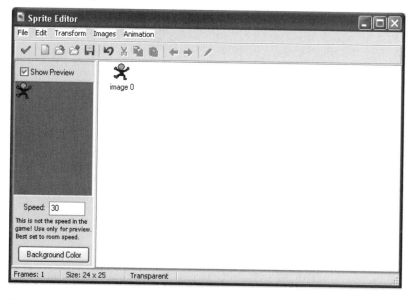

FIGURE 12.8   Animated gif sequence showing Robo running to the left.

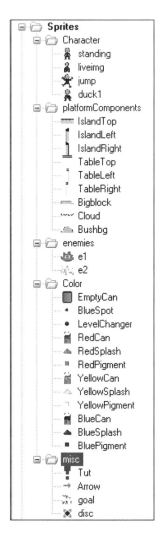

FIGURE 12.9   Other sprites used.

CREATING THE ROOMS

As mentioned earlier, the game rooms used in platform games are typically very large. Figure 12.10 shows the room configuration details for the Tutorial room. It has been created to be 2000 pixels wide and 199 pixels high. What you see on the screen is only a portion of the complete room. This room is quite a long room. It extends beyond the width of most computer screens.

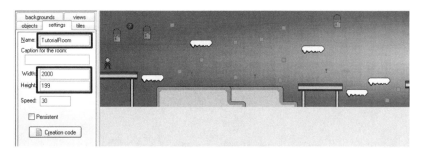

FIGURE 12.10   Room size setting for the platform room.

After creating the room, we can assign it an appropriate background using either a digital photograph or a digital picture made with graphical editors on a computer. If the picture is too small, you can stretch it by checking the Stretch box shown in Figure 12.11. You can also tile the picture horizontally and vertically to fill up the room. You can see all the other selected options we used to create our room's background highlighted in Figure 12.11

For our extra-long room, the most important options to configure are found under the View tab of the Room properties window. Defining a view provides a mechanism to define a rectangular area within the extra-long room that is visible to the player. We would like the user to initially be able to see only this portion of the room. This small area is called a *view,* which is basically a rectangular area of the room visible to the user. As such, a view has to be described using dimensions needed to define a rectangle. This needs four values. The view's X and Y coordinates specify its top-left corner. These coordinates are measured relative to the top- left corner of the room. The other two values are the room width and the room height, which specify the dimensions of the room.

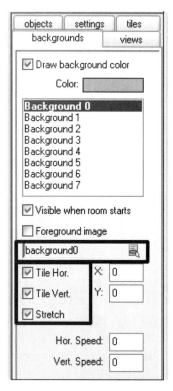

FIGURE 12.11 Background options.

The first setting that needs to be configured is to enable the use of views in the View tab of the Room properties window. Figure 12.12 shows the View tab with the Enable the Use of Views option turned off on the top left corner. We also need to make the view visible when the room starts. This is done by checking the option labeled Visible When Room Starts.

Figure 12.12 also provides two example views and the configuration settings for each. View 1 is the larger view. Its top left corner coordinates, X and Y, are both zero. It's width is 200 and height is 199. View 2 is the smaller view. Its top left corner coordinates X and Y are both 50. Its height and width are both 50 units.

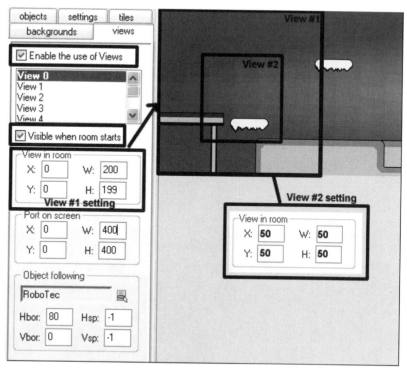

FIGURE 12.12   View options.

You may notice that View 1 occupies the complete room height, so there is no need to scroll in the vertical direction. View 1 takes only 10% of the room width, so there is a lot of room to scroll horizontally. View 2 occupies 50 pixels in height and width. If you were making a game using View 2, you would need to be able to scroll both horizontally and vertically.

After defining the view size, we need to define the Scroller object. The Scroller object is configured by identifying the object of your choice in the drop-down box labeled Object Following shown on the lower-left corner of Figure 12.12. This is the object that the Game Engine uses and tracks to update the view. The Engine tries to keep this object visible at all times. If the player moves this object close to the right boundary of the view, the Game Engine will scroll the view to the right so that the Scroller object does not leave the view. Figure 12.13 shows how the view changes as the Scroller object moves to the right.

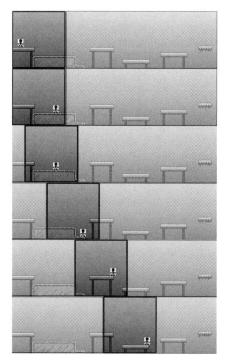

FIGURE 12.13 The Scroller object and the corresponding view at different locations.

In Figure 12.13, the user only sees the highlighted square with the little person inside. The dimmed out portions of the room are only shown for clarity. The Game Engine keeps the dimmed out portions hidden from the user. This highlighted square and its contents are shown on a window of fixed size on a fixed location on the screen. Figure 12.13 is a conceptual diagram of how a view is displayed and how it changes with the motion of the Scroller object.

The size of the window displayed on screen can be configured using the same Views tab of the Room Configuration window. The size of the view on the screen can be configured by setting the four values for the Port on Screen subwindow shown in Figure 12.14. This setting allows you to magnify the view, shrink the view, or show it the same size. If the setting in the View in Room section matches the values in the Port on Screen section, the size of the view and the screen size of the image will be the same. In the example shown in Figure 12.14, the Port on Screen setting is double that of the View in Room setting. This magnifies the view by a factor of two and makes the user see a larger view on the screen. You could similarly shrink the view and display a compressed view on the screen by using smaller values in the Port on Screen subwindow.

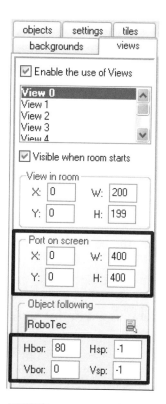

FIGURE 12.14 Configuring the screen's View Port.

One last setting needs to be configured in the View tab of the Room properties window shown on the lower-left corner of Figure 12.14. This setting is the values for Hbor and Vbor. The Hbor and Vbor values are the border size in pixels that we would like to keep visible around the Scroller object as it moves. Think of these values as an incremental height and width component for the Scroller object. These two values create a virtual Scroller object that is bigger than the real one. The game engine attempts to use this virtual Scroller object when it adjusts the views. If it gets close to the edge of the room, it may not be possible to maintain these values. A bigger value of Hbor would result in a large virtual Scroller and the scrolling would start when you are farther away from the edge. If you assigned smaller values, the virtual Scroller object would be smaller and will need to get closer to the edge to scroll the view.

DESIGNING THE GAME OBJECTS

In this section, we'll look at how platform game objects are designed. Several categories of objects are required for the game. They are:

- Color objects
- Tutorial objects
- Enemy objects
- Platform objects
- Player objects
- Miscellaneous objects

The color objects encapsulate all the work related to picking up color and receiving points. This includes handling logic for paint cans, paint pigments, paint splashes, and empty paint cans. We need a set of platform objects that are used to create the platform. This includes the creation of objects related to high platforms, ground planes, clouds, and more. We have a set of tutorial objects that provide small pieces of information about the game. The objects in the enemy category include all the objects that could harm the player. The objects in the miscellaneous category include all those objects that do not fit into any of the above categories. The one object that was not placed in any category is the Robo object. This is the object the player controls. This object can jump across platforms, collect paint blocks, smash open paint cans, kill enemies, and more. Now let's look at these objects in more detail.

THE COLOR OBJECTS

The color objects correspond to treasure in a traditional game and are the objects that the player attempts to collect during the game. There are red, yellow, and blue color objects. For each color, there are three subcategories of objects: the pigment object, the splash object, and the paint can object. The RedPaintCan object, for example, contains five pints of red paint. The Robo object can knock it over from underneath to earn five points. When the RedPaintCan object is knocked over, it creates an instance of a RedSplash object. The RedSplash object is an animation that provides a visual clue to the player, depicting the emptying of a paint can. Apart from the RedPaintCan object and the RedSplash object, there is the RedPigment object, which can be collected for one point.

The RedPigment object inherits properties from the ParentPigment objects. The ParentPigment object awards the player one point and destroys itself when it collides with the Robo object. Since the parent object does all the work, the RedPigment object does not have any events or actions in its property windows. Figure 12.15 shows the hierarchy of the pigment objects.

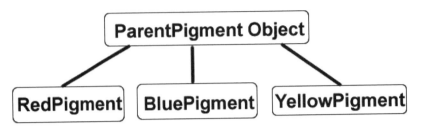

FIGURE 12.15 Pigment objects hierarchy.

The `RedPaintCan` object is responsible for creating the `RedSplash` object. The `Step` event of the `RedPaintCan` object is shown in Figure 12.16. The first highlighted box shows the action that checks to see if the `Robo` object is on the verge of colliding with the `RedPaintCan` object. The second highlighted action creates an instance of the `RedSplash` object. The player is awarded five points just below that. The third highlighted action converts the `RedPaintCan` into an `EmptyPaintCan`.

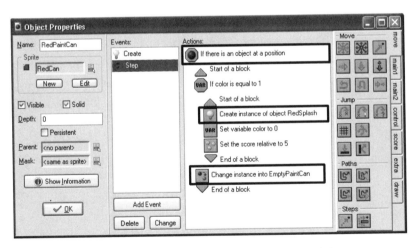

FIGURE 12.16 Actions executed during the `Step` Event of the RedPaintCan.

The splash objects are similar to the pigment objects. Splash objects of all colors have common characteristics that have been extracted and encapsulated in a `ParentSplash` object. The `ParentSplash` object sets the lifetime of the object to

20 steps using an alarm. After the execution of 20 steps, the player is awarded one point and the instance is destroyed. The hierarchy of splash objects is shown in Figure 12.17.

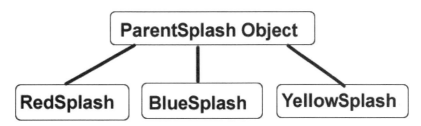

FIGURE 12.17   Splash object hierarchy.

THE TUTORIAL OBJECTS

The tutorial objects provide the user game playing instructions and tips. Using tutorial objects, we can quickly receive pieces of information in an incremental fashion at different times during the game. In The Color Game, these objects display a message when the Robo object collides against them. Since all tutorial objects deliver different messages but exhibit the same behavior, they all inherit actions and events from a ParentTutorial object that encapsulates their common behavior.

When the game begins, the Start object found on the first screen sets up a global variable called tutorial. It is set to a value of one if the user requests tutorials, as shown in Figure 12.18. Otherwise, the value is set to zero.

FIGURE 12.18   Setting the global variable called tutorial.

The tutorial objects in this game have a little inbuilt intelligence and can switch to become a `BluePigment` object if required. That sounds complicated, but it is very simple to implement. If the user does not need tutorials, the global variable tutorial is set to zero. All tutorial objects inherit the characteristics of the `ParentTutorial` object. The `Parent-Tutorial` object checks whether the global variable `tutorial` is set to zero, as shown in Figure 12.19, and converts the tutorial objects into `BluePigment` objects if no tutorials are required. If you open up the tutorial room, you will see several tutorial objects placed at vantage points. These objects become `BluePigment` objects if tutorials are not required.

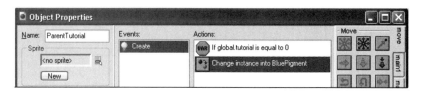

FIGURE 12.19   Checking the global variable called `tutorial`.

The behavior of tutorial objects is very simple. They respond to collision events with the `Robo` object, display the message embedded in them, and then destroy themselves after the user acknowledges reading the message by pressing the OK button on the pop-up dialog box. Here are the messages displayed by each of the tutorial objects.

Tutorial #1

"Welcome! As you can see, the world is dull and there is very little color left. You have been sent to retrieve all the color. Collect the color pigments along your way to make the world a wonderful place to live. You can walk along the long corridor to the right to find interesting places to discover!"

Tutorial #2

"You may have noticed that pressing the left and right arrow keys moves you in either direction. You can jump by pressing the spacebar. You can also jump left and jump right using a combination of the jump and arrow keys together: that will help you collect color pigments that are above your head!"

Tutorial #3

"Try to pick up all the floating blocks of color as you move around to make your world colorful! You can find more color in the next level after you finish exploring this level."

Tutorial #4

"Keep following the red arrows. You will loose a life if you fall into crevices! So do not try to pick up color in dangerous places!"

Tutorial #5

"Now here is a secret you should know! If you press the down arrow and then press the spacebar simultaneously, you can jump much higher. Try it out! Go back, jump higher, and pick up color blocks you could not reach earlier!"

Tutorial #6

"Don't be afraid to walk on empty paint cans. They can help you reach new areas."

Tutorial #7

"You may have noticed that you get one point for every color you picked up. There are also cans of paint that you could break open. You get five points by jumping underneath paint cans and breaking them. Try it out!"

Now that we know how the tutorial objects let's, look at the most important character in our game—the Robo object.

THE Robo **OBJECT**

The Robo object, also known as the Scroller object, is the one that is controlled by the player. It is the object that embeds most of the game logic. It responds to left, right, and down arrow keys, as well as the spacebar. The action that makes the Robo an interesting object is the Set Gravity action. If the Robo is in the air, the gravity is set to a value of 0.6. If it collides with any platform element or a paint can, its gravity is reset to zero. Gravity is set and reset in the Step event, as shown in Figure 12.20.

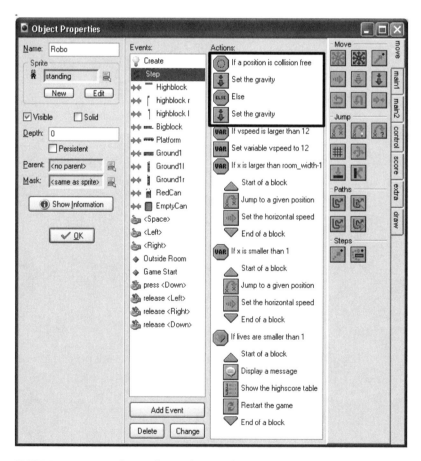

FIGURE 12.20 Setting and resetting gravity.

A variable called `highjump` is initialized to zero when the Robo is created. This value is set to one when the down arrow is pressed and reset to zero once again when the down arrow is released. Pressing the spacebar makes the Robo jump up. If the variable `highjump` is set to one, the speed with which the Robo moves is higher, resulting in a higher jump. While jumping, the sprite is changed to depict a jumping pose. All the actions used to make Robo jump during the Spacebar keyboard event are shown in Figure 12.21.

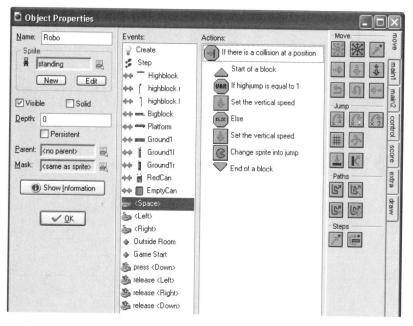

FIGURE 12.21   Actions executed during the Spacebar keyboard event.

ENEMY OBJECTS

In The Color Game, we have one example of an enemy object called poison. If the Robo collides against this object, the player looses one life. There are just two events the poison object responds to: collision with the Robo and collision with the disc.

The disc is a projectile launched by the Robo. Pressing the Z key launches a projectile in the direction in which the Robo is traveling.

One can create many types of enemies to make the game harder to play. You could have enemies that are not destroyed by one hit from a projectile, but by several shots. You could have tall and wide enemies that you have to jump across. You could have enemies moving up and down based on a timeline that makes it hard for the player to incapacitate them.

FINAL THOUGHTS

Platform games are not only fun to play, but they are easy to create. You can make your own platform games that are very similar to the commercial versions available in retail stores. Using the platform game provided in the Game Maker file example12.1.gm6 as a template, you should be able to create a customized platform game and give it to a friend as a birthday present.

ON THE CD

SUMMARY

In this chapter we learned to create platform games. The game room design is the key concept here. A large room that usually extends beyond the size of the screen is created and a small window into this room is presented as a view to the player. We created an object that controls the location of the scrolling window. When this object get close to designated edges, the window into the room scrolls providing the illusion of motion to the player. Remember, the Scroller object is just another regular object that is defined in the Views tab of the game room Properties window, as shown in Figure 12.12. This is the object the game engine keeps track of to scroll the view. The Port on Screen parameters in the views tab defines the size of the view visible to the player.

We also looked at building sprites using basic components that could be assembled together to create bigger sprites, and we looked at animated sprites once again. We introduced the concept of providing basic tutorials on how to play the game using tutorial objects that provide the player incremental information about the rules of the game.

Project

As an additional exercise, using the concepts learned in this chapter, create a platform game using a vertical scroller. An appropriate theme would be to explore an underground gold mine, pick up the treasure and bring it back to the top. Create nice background images that have caves and dark passageways. Gold nuggets could be created using animated sprites.

CHAPTER 13

Tips and Tricks

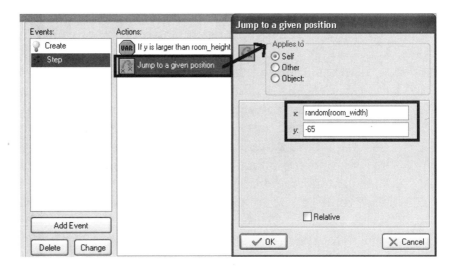

In this chapter:

- Scrolling Shooters
- Implementing Shooters
- Car Game
- Conclusion

In this chapter, we'll look at a couple of different strategies used to create games. Rather than creating games from scratch, we will be learning by example, which is a productive way to learn new concepts. All the games used in this chapter were installed for you automatically when you installed the Game Maker software using the instructions provided in Chapter 1.

The motivation for the format of this chapter came from the experience of looking through different books while learning various programming languages. The basic premise is that learning is an active process that ideally should be engaging, but there are different ways to achieve this goal. Some books on programming languages provide information on all the grammar and language constructs in detail and then teach you to create your own programs. The philosophy of such a method is that you need to know all the rules of the game before you start playing. Other books start with a simple program and then incrementally build on that. Here the philosophy is that the rules of the game will be provided to you as you need them and when you are ready for them. When there are many rules in a game, the latter approach is usually much easier.

With that in mind, we'll start looking at fully functional working games and learn by example. Before looking at the source code, we'll play the game first. This will set aside some time for our inquisitive minds to gather information and facilitate attempts to discover some of the infrastructural elements used to create the game. This will help us build a repertoire of lifelong skills that will prove helpful for designing and building new games in the future. This book was not designed for the passive reader, but rather for seekers of enjoyable hands-on intellectual enrichment. We will therefore use engaging examples to look at what Game Maker can do for you. It is much easier to see working examples and then learn about the objects, rooms, actions, and events used to create them. Let's get started.

SCROLLING SHOOTERS

In this last chapter, we'll look at the techniques used to make traditional arcade games. We will look at games that are complete by themselves and investigate some of the tips and tricks used to create these games. The first category of games we will look at are termed scrolling shooters. Games such as *Space Invaders* and *Car Racers* belong to this category, where a moving background scrolls vertically, horizontally, or in both directions. Unlike the platform game depicted in Figure 12.13, scrolling shooters do not use scrolling views of large rooms. Backgrounds used in scrolling shooters are typically digital pictures that depict the appropriate surroundings for the game. These digital pictures are made to move by assigning them a vertical and/or a horizontal speed to provide a dynamic look and feel. The game designer creates different kinds of sprites and objects that could be overlaid on this background. Think of this as a two-layered system in which the lower layer has the background and the upper layer has the objects. Let's use an example to understand the inner workings of a scrolling shooter.

Let's open up the game found in the Game Maker examples directory. If you installed Game Maker using the default installation directory, you will find it at the location C:\Program Files\Game_Maker6\Examples\1945.gm6. If you installed it elsewhere, navigate to the appropriate directory and open up that file. Using the File > Open command, open the Game Maker file 1945.gm6 found in the examples directory.

Take a minute to play the game. Use the arrow keys to move your plane around and press the spacebar to shoot the enemies down.

You may have noticed that the plane flies over a blue ocean with isolated islands at different locations. Look again and you may notice that you plane is not moving, but instead the background beneath the plane is moving. This moving background provides an illusion for the players that the object they control is moving. Let's see how this was done. Let's close the game and expand the Backgrounds tab. Let's open up the property window for the background resource named back_water, as shown in Figure 13.1.

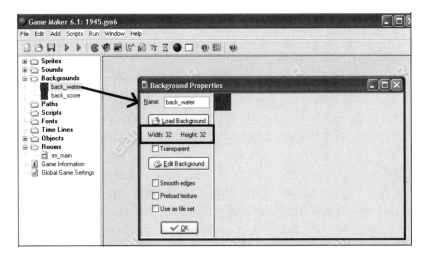

FIGURE 13.1 Opening the background resource.

You will notice in the highlighted rectangle that the size of the image used for the background is 32 pixels wide and 32 pixels high. To create an ocean, these images will have to be placed in several rows and columns next to each other. This can be done using the Backgrounds tab of the Room Properties window. Let's open up the room properties shown in Figure 13.2 by double-clicking on the room called rm_main found under the Rooms Resource section.

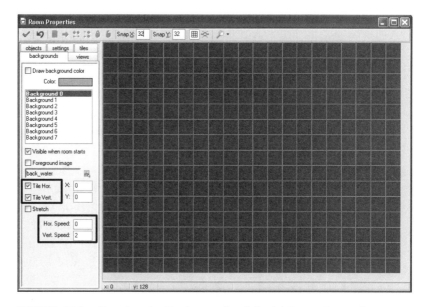

FIGURE 13.2   Opening the Backgrounds tab in the Room Properties window.

On the right side you will notice that the back_water background image has been laid out in several rows and columns. This has been done automatically for us since we have the Horizontal and Vertical Tiling options enabled in the box highlighted on the lower-left corner of Figure 13.2. You can uncheck different combinations of these two options to understand how the tiling of images is accomplished. After you are done trying that out, put the settings back to what they were originally. The other highlighted box in Figure 13.2 shows the setting for the background's vertical and horizontal speed. The vertical speed is two and the horizontal speed is zero. This means that all the tiny back_water pictures that make up the background move down two pixels at a time. Empty spaces that appear at the top on the screen as a result of all the images moving down are filled up with new back_water images. You can visualize this as a set of tiny back_water images embarking on a journey that starts at the top of the screen and ends at the bottom. After they reach they bottom, they get teleported to the starting point at the top of the screen and restart their journey. This cycle of images moving around provides an illusion of motion.

Overlaying moving islands and other realistic entities over the ocean can enhance this illusion of motion. We could have drawn islands in our background and made them move around, but that would create the appearance of the islands predictable since the images follow a fixed path. The game would become boring if you knew when and where an island would appear. Let's look at a different mechanism to do this. We'll be using intelligent island objects that appear at random locations from the top of the screen. Open up one of the island objects found under the Objects Resource section of the Resource Explorer. Double-click `obj_island1` to open up the Object Properties window, as shown in Figure 13.3.

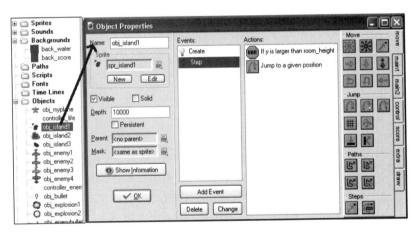

FIGURE 13.3   Object Properties window for `obj_island1`.

If you look at the `Create` event for this island, you will notice that there is just one action that sets the vertical speed to two pixels per step. This is the same speed as that of the background shown in Figure 13.2. Since the background and the island move at the same speed, it will create an illusion that they both are one large ocean and landmass entity.

What happens when the island reaches the bottom of the screen? We could make it appear back at the top of the screen along the same vertical path after it has completed its journey. This would make the appearance of islands a predictable event resulting in a monotonous game. Let's examine the actions on the right side of Figure 13.3. The first action checks to see if the island has reached the bottom of the room. If it has crossed the lower boundary of the room, we execute a jump action. Let's open the properties box for the Jump action highlighted in Figure 13.4.

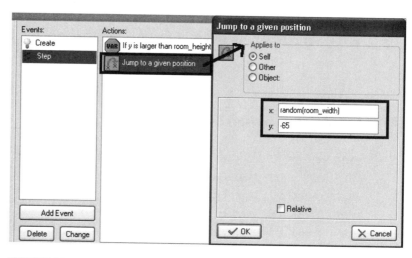

FIGURE 13.4   Properties window for Jump action.

You will notice that the object is programmed to jump to a new location whose X coordinate is defined as random(room_width). This is a Game Maker function that generates a random number that is a number between zero and room_width. The global variable that holds the width of the room is appropriately named room_width. A X coordinate of –65 moves the island 65 pixels above the top of the room. This is done to ensure that the island is completely above the upper edge of the room before it starts its journey. Moving it

closer to the edge may result in a little part of the island becoming abruptly visible.

We now have an island object that scrolls down and appears randomly from the top of the screen. If you look all the
island objects, you will see a similar behavior. When all these
objects are put together in a room, we get a nice scrolling
background that is not monotonous.

Open the properties windows for any of the enemy aircraft. You will notice that they too use the same technique
described in the previous few paragraphs except that they are
created with a speed of four pixels per step. That is double the
speed of the ocean and islands. This provides the illusion of
a very fast enemy aircraft that flies toward the bottom of the
screen.

IMPLEMENTING SHOOTERS

Shooters were described earlier in the section on projectiles
in Chapter 6. In this game, the player controls the object
named obj_myplane. Let's open up its Properties window by
double-clicking on obj_myplane in the resource tree. Let's
look at the actions for the Left keyboard event, as shown in
Figure 13.5. The first action checks to see if the object's X coordinate is greater than 40. The second action is a Jump action. On inspecting the Jump action's Property window, you
will notice that the object would move minus four pixels in
the x direction. This is the same as moving four pixels to the
left. What these two actions do together is to allow the object
to move to the left four pixels at a time as long as it is at least
40 pixels away from the left edge of the room. This ensures
that the plane you control has a limit on how far it can move
to the left.

You will see similar actions for the keyboard event that
occurs when you press the right-arrow key. That puts a limit
on how far your plane can move to the right. These limitations have been put in place so that the plane does not get lost

when it moves outside the room. Some games do not place this limitation and instead use a wrap-around mechanism to bring objects that leave the screen on one side to magically appear on the other end. It is totally up to the game designer to decide on that.

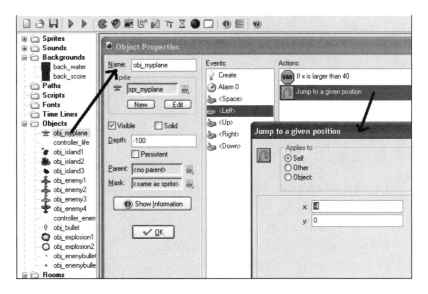

FIGURE 13.5   Properties window for the player's plane object.

Now that we know how the user controls the plane, let's explore techniques to shoot projectiles at the enemy using the Spacebar event. Let's open the actions for the Spacebar event, as shown in Figure 13.6. The first action you'll see on the right is a check that determines if a variable named can_shoot is set to a value of one. This variable acts like a gatekeeper. The object named my_plane can shoot projectiles only if this variable is set to a value of one. The can_shoot gatekeeper variable is set to zero in one of the actions found close to the bottom of the action list in Figure 13.6. If the player presses the spacebar at such a time, the plane will not shoot projectiles. To enable shooting, someone has to set the can_shoot gatekeeper variable to a value of one.

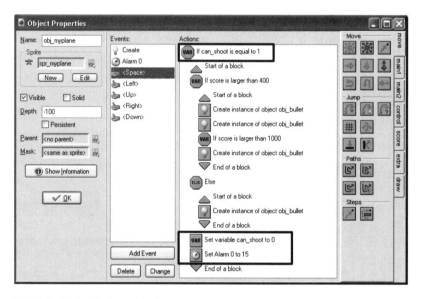

FIGURE 13.6   Actions for the Spacebar event.

The can_shoot variable is set to one by an alarm event. The second to last action in Figure 13.6 sets Alarm 0 to 15. After an interval of 15 game steps (or about half a second), an alarm event is generated. If you open up the actions executed by the obj_myplane object during the Alarm 0 event, you will see an action that sets the can_shoot variable to a value of one. After this action is executed, you should be able to press the spacebar and shoot again.

If we did not have an alarm-based mechanism to turn the can_shoot variable on and off, the object would fire shots very fast like a machine gun. This would make the game less challenging. If we modify the Set Alarm action shown in Figure 13.6 to a larger setting, for example, Set Alarm 0 to 30, then the plane will be able to create projectiles once every 30 steps (that is every second). This could make the player's plane vulnerable to attack and make the game too hard to play. The setting for the alarm is critical in achieving the right game play.

Also note that Figure 13.6 shows actions that check the number of points accumulated by the player. If the player's score is less that 400, one bullet object is created during a Spacebar event. Two bullets are created if the score is greater than 400. A score of 1000 or more results in the creation of three bullets.

Now that we understand the key components that make up the game, you can try some of the small projects listed below and make your own custom game.

- Make the player's airplane more agile. It should move faster to the left and right.
- Change the scoring so that you get more points.
- Make the player get to a score of 1000 in an easier and faster way.
- Make the plane shoot bullets at a faster rate.

CAR GAME

Now let's look at another kind of game. This is a completely working version of a car driving game. Your goal is to drive the car and avoid crashing into traffic traveling in either direction. At random locations you will find gasoline. This needs to be picked up to keep your car running. This game also can be modified, and there are a couple of neat tricks used in the game.

Let's open up the Street Race game found in the Game Maker examples directory. If you installed Game Maker using the default installation directory, you will find it at the location C:\Program Files\Game_Maker6\Examples\street ON THE CD race.gm6. If you installed it elsewhere, navigate to the appropriate directory and open up that file. Using the File > Open command, open the Game Maker file street race.gm6 found in the examples directory. Take a minute to play the game. You control the red car. The up, down, left, and right keys can be used to move your car around. Your goal is to avoid crashing your car. You also need to fill up on gas if you see gas objects while driving. Play for a while and then close the game. Let's look at some of the components that make up the game.

Let's open the game room named room1. Figure 13.7 shows the geometry and dimensions of the room. The upper-left corner has its X and Y coordinates set to zero. It is the origin. The lower-right corner has the X coordinate set to 400 and the Y coordinate set to 475. Each lane is 60 pixels wide and the cars are 40 pixels wide.

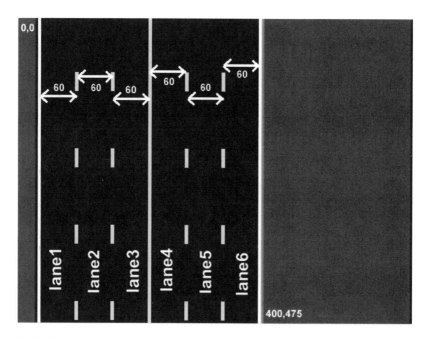

FIGURE 13.7 Room1 geometry.

Let's open up the objects portion of the resource tree. There are two controller objects, four cars, and one gas object. Let's look at the object named controller to start with. It creates all the car objects that drive up and down the lanes and the gas object that one finds randomly on the street. The Create event sets an alarm using the Set Alarm 0 to 300 action. The Alarm 0 event and the actions executed are shown in Figure 13.8. The actions on the right create an instance of the gas object and then set the alarm back on. The alarm is reset using a value that is calculated by adding 300 to a percentage of the score. This makes it harder to find gas objects as your score goes higher. It will take longer for a gas object to be created with higher scores. You could use this technique anytime you want a game to get harder with higher scores!

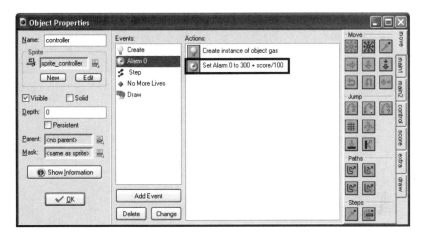

FIGURE 13.8   Actions for the Alarm event.

Let's look at the Step event now. This is where all the car objects get created. We want the car objects to be created randomly to provide an element of surprise for the player. This is done using the Chance action that simulates the throwing of a die. It simulates a real die but is better than a real die since it could have any number of sides. Chance actions always have another action following them. If throwing the die yields the one lying face up, the action that follows the Chance action is executed. Figure 13.9 shows the actions executed during a Step event for the controller object. Highlighted in the same figure you can see the use of a Chance action and a Create action that follows it.

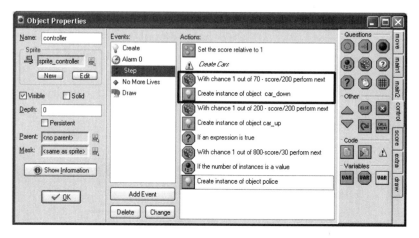

FIGURE 13.9 Actions for the Step event.

In this example, an attempt is made to create an instance of the object named car_down based on the result of throwing a die. The larger the number of sides on the die, the less likely the event will happen. The chances of a car_down object being created depends on the result of throwing a die that has about 70 sides. At the bottom of the action list in Figure 13.9, you will see that the chances of creating a police car object depends on the results of throwing an 800-sided dice.

The dice-throwing logic is also used to position a car in one of six lanes and to set its speed. Let's look at actions for the Create event of the car_down object shown in Figure 13.10. You will notice two highlighted chance actions. The upper Chance action rolls a die with two sides, so the chance of executing the actions that follow is 50%. The other Chance action has a 33% probability of triggering the actions that follow. This action resets the speed and location for the new car.

We have looked at several situations in which the Chance action can be used. You now have this additional trick to add to your skill set to create and control game assets at random intervals of time.

Let's look at one more action that is very useful when you want to draw a lot of custom graphics. Let's open the controller_start object in the street race game. This object

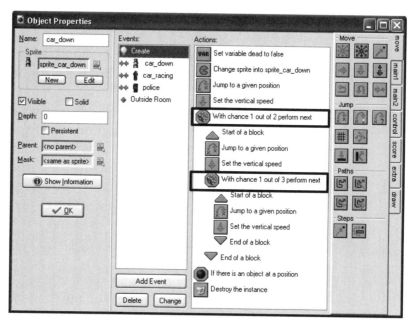

FIGURE 13.10   Chance actions in the Create event.

responds to four events. The AnyKey event is useful when you want something to be done when any key on the keyboard has been pressed. We looked at the Game Start and Step events in earlier chapters. The Draw action is one that is of interest to us.

We need to understand a little bit about game engines and how they work before we look at the Draw event. We know that every game is made up of one or more game objects. Each of these game objects needs to do different things based on external events such as mouse clicks or keyboard events and more. The Game Engine ensures that all objects do things in an orderly manner. The Game Engine first decides on a frame rate at which the screen will be refreshed. For example, it could be 30 times a second or 15 frames a second. If the screen is refreshed at a very slow speed of two frames per second we would be able to see all the jerky motion of the game objects. If the frame rate is higher than 18 frames per second, the human eye cannot see each individual frame and therefore sees continuity in motion like a motion picture.

Depending on the frame rate of the game, the Game Engine decides on a frequency at which all the objects should be given an opportunity to do their own tasks. For a frame rate of 30 frames per second, each object needs to be serviced by the Game Engine and given a chance to draw itself on the screen 30 times a second. When the object is given a chance to draw itself and do other tasks, it needs to finish that as quickly as possible since there could be many other objects waiting to be serviced by the Game Engine. The Game Engine acts as the controller and provides a preemptive time-slicing mechanism to make sure all objects behave fairly and do not hog up all the time.

Every object also has an opportunity to respond to a Draw event. This event can be used by a game object to draw something special on the screen. It usually draws an image of itself using custom graphic functions. Let's look at the Draw event for the controller_start object shown in Figure 13.11.

This draw event is generated by the Game Engine at frequent intervals of time and it provides an opportunity for the controller_start object to draw something on the screen. In this case, the opportunity is used to set a custom font and color and then write the text "Street Racing" on the screen. The font and color are then changed once again and two text lines are drawn using the Draw a Text action. Inspect all the actions—they are all self-explanatory. You now have the ability to control what is drawn on the screen by handling the Draw event for objects.

Before we end this chapter, we'd like to point you to a couple of locations to pick up some good editable games. Now that you have a good understanding of Game Maker, it is a good time to look at some of these games. Most of them require scripting, but now you should be ready to plunge into it.

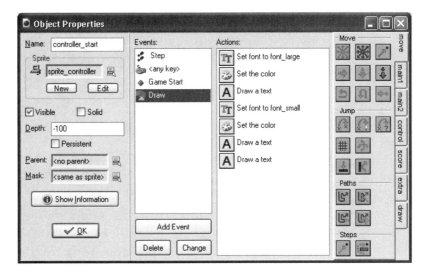

FIGURE 13.11   Draw event.

EDITABLE GAMES

Here is a list of editable games you could find at *http://www.gamemaker.nl/games_edit6.html*. Note that the copyright and full responsibility for these games rest with the creators.

***Version 6.0 Demos*, written by Mark Overmars:** This file contains some demos for version 6.1—the registration features demo, the particle demo, and the effect demo. (These demos only work in version 6.1 of Game Maker.)

***Legend of Mana*, written by Roderik Boerma:** A RPG/adventure game in which you must reclaim the mana seed that was taken away by your dog. To do so you must fight the enemies. A nice touch is that your strength must recharge after every hit, so hitting lots of times in a row is not going to help much. This game was written as the final assignment for the game design course at Utrecht University.

***Cursed Undead*, written by Nees Sonnemans:** As a cursed undead, you fight through the dangerous levels of a dark dungeon filled with monsters in order to defeat and become the Undead Lord. This game was written as the final assignment for the game design course at Utrecht University.

MARS: Final Conflict, **written by Arjen Swart and Akil Kömür:** Real-time strategy (RTS) game in space, with four levels. As in any RTS game, you must build a base and set up your defenses. The tasks in the levels are rather different. This game was written as the final assignment for the game design course at Utrecht University.

Yet Another Zelda, written by Roderik Heij and Tim Adelaar: A Zelda type of game. Very well done with a number of different levels. One hint: get the boomerang before trying to catch the chickens. This game was written as the final assignment for the game design course at Utrecht University.

Commando and Conquistare, **written by Joost Vermeulen and Roel van der Kraan:** A sort of standard RTS game in the style of *Command and Conquer,* in which the player must construct a base and attack and defeat the enemy. This game was written as the final assignment for the game design course at Utrecht University.

The Dark Age, **written by Michiel Mastenbroek and Sander Smid:** A RTS game that is a bit of a mix of *Settlers* and *Warcraft.* Players must collect resources, build a settlement, produce weapons, and conquer the enemy. This game was written as the final assignment for the game design course at Utrecht University.

The Blue Lady, **written by Gabor de Mooij:** A great adventure game. A very friendly game with nice graphics, interesting puzzles, and great music by Bjorn Lynne. Requires a registered version of Game Maker.

Bacteria, **written by Simon Donkers:** A wonderful but difficult puzzle game. The goal is simply to destroy all red stones by connecting them to your green stones, but it is way more complicated than it seems and the computer opponent is very strong. Requires a registered version of Game Maker.

Registered Demo Features, **written by Mark Overmars:** This is a demonstration program showing a number of the registered-only features in Game Maker 6.0. In particular, it gives examples of advanced drawing functions, motion planning, positional sound, and 3D functionality. As a bonus it contains a little first person shooter game (but you only have to shoot logos—no enemies). (This demo does not work under version 6.1 of Game Maker.)

Breakout, **written by Mark Overmars:** A very basic version of breakout. It is a simple example game that you are free to edit and use any way you like.

Life, **written by Mark Overmars:** The classic game of life. It is a very simple example game that you are free to edit and use any way you like.

SUMMARY

In this chapter we explored a couple of tips for creating different kinds of games, and analyzed an example of a scrolling shooter game. We looked at mechanisms to simulate motion by moving the background instead of the player, and we moved objects randomly back to a starting location, if they scrolled past the bottom of the room.

Project

As an exercise, look through the games mentioned in this chapter. Some of them required the knowledge of more advanced concepts in scripting. You may now be interested in unlocking the advanced features of Game Maker, which requires you to register the product for a nominal fee at *http://www.gamemaker.nl.* If you choose to do this, you will get a whole set of new features that could be used to create exciting games!

About the CD-ROM

The companion CD-ROM is packed with everything you need to make all of the games in this book and the free version of the Game Maker 6.1 software development tool.

GENERAL MINIMUM SYSTEM REQUIREMENTS FOR GAME MAKER 6.1

To install Game Maker 6.1, you will need a computer that can run Windows 98 or better with a CD-ROM drive, sound card, and mouse.

Game Maker runs only on Windows, versions 98 SE, 2000, ME, XP (and later). It does require a DirectX 8 or higher compatible graphics card with at least 16MB of video memory (preferably 32MB or more). Also a DirectX 8 or higher compatible sound card is required. More details of this software can be found at the website *http://www. gamemaker.nl/index.html*

CONTENTS OF CD

The CD is organized into a set of directories as shown below.

- Table of Contents
- Acknowledgements
- Introduction
- Chapter 1 – contains example and figures used in this chapter
- Chapter 2 – contains example and figures used in this chapter
- Chapter 3 – contains example and figures used in this chapter
- Chapter 4 – contains example and figures used in this chapter
- Chapter 5 – contains example and figures used in this chapter

- Chapter 6 – contains example and figures used in this chapter
- Chapter 7 – contains example and figures used in this chapter
- Chapter 8 – contains example and figures used in this chapter
- Chapter 9 – contains example and figures used in this chapter
- Chapter 10 – contains example and figures used in this chapter
- Chapter 11 – contains example and figures used in this chapter
- Chapter 12 – contains example and figures used in this chapter
- Chapter 13 – contains example and figures used in this chapter
- Resources – images and videos
    - Backgrounds – background images
    - Sound – sound files used in examples
    - Sprites – sprites used in examples
- Application
    - Gmaker.exe – is the Installable Game Maker Executable

ADDITIONAL INFORMATION

The free version of the Game Maker software is contained on this CD-ROM. The free version can be upgraded for a nominal fee to the Full Version. The full version of Game Maker has a number of important extra features, in particular:

- No *Game Maker* logo when running a game.
- Rotated, color blended, and translucent sprites.
- Additional actions for e.g., CD music, rotated text, and colorized shapes.
- Special sound effects and positional sound.
- A number of advanced drawing functions, e.g. for textured polygons.

- A particle system to create fireworks, flames, rain, and other effects.
- Functions for 3D graphics.
- The possibility of making multiplayer games that can be played over a network.
- Functions to create and modify resources (sprites, backgrounds, etc.) while the game is running.
- A collection of functions to create and use data structures.
- Functions for motion planning.
- The possibility of extending Game Maker using DLLs.

The Key Positions in a Development Team

As was previously mentioned, a development project is made up several key positions. Without any of these, it would not be successful. That being said, depending on the size of your team, a single individual may be forced to wear many hats, or in the case of the lone developer, all of the hats. That is, although all of the positions are required, a single individual may fill one or all of them.

Because the game industry is still in its infancy, it's sometimes difficult to discuss the positions that make up a team. The type of game being produced definitely has a profound effect on the required personnel. Every development project is arranged differently. As the industry matures, there will certainly be more standard types of arrangements. But until that occurs, we are stuck trying to explain most of the potential positions.

DESIGNER

Many development projects have a lead game designer who is responsible for the creation of the game script. However, this position is often one of the most misunderstood of any of the key positions and is often left completely off the team. This leaves room for everyone, from the producer to programmers, clamoring for the title.

It is the designer who makes many of the decisions related to the creation of important aspects such as puzzles or the levels in a first person shooter. Like a screenwriter for a movie, the designer is responsible for the overall feel of the game. Communication is a very important aspect of this job, as designers work with the other team members throughout the duration of a project.

In the beginning stages of a game, designers spend most of their time focusing on writing short scripts and working on the beginning storyboard sketches. A typical storyboard displays the action of a game, in a very simple manner. Depending on the basic talents of the designer, the storyboard may even include stick figures and basic shapes to convey the action. Storyboards are a sort of rough draft that will later be transformed into the game itself.

After the decisions have been made on the game concepts, the designers begin working on a blueprint for the game called a *design document*. Simply put, the document details every aspect of a game and will evolve as the game is being developed.

PROGRAMMER

Game programmers are software developers who take the ideas, art, and music and combine them into a software project. Programmers obviously write the code for the game, but they may also have several additional responsibilities. For instance, if an artist is designing graphics for the game, the lead programmer could be responsible for the development of a custom set of tools for creating the graphics. It is also the lead programmer's job to keep everything running smoothly and to somehow figure out a way to satisfy everyone, from the producer to the artists. Unlike the stereotype portrayed on many Web sites, books, or even movies, programmers usually don't stroll into work at noon, work for a few hours, and then leave. The truth is that they often arrive earlier and leave later than anyone else on the development team.

Programmers are responsible for taking the vast number of elements and combining them to form the executable program. They decide how fast characters can run and how high they can jump. They are responsible for accounting for everything inside of the virtual world. While doing all of this, they often will attempt to create software that can be reusable for other projects, and spend a great deal of time optimizing the code to make it is as fast as possible.

Sometimes a given project may have several programmers who specialize in one key area, such as graphics, sound, or artificial intelligence (AI). The following list details the various types of programmers and what they are primarily responsible for:

Engine or Graphics Programmers: they create the software that controls how graphics and animations are stored and ultimately displayed on the screen.

AI Programmers: they create a series of rules that determine how enemies or characters will react to game situations and attempt to make them act as realistically as possible.

Sound Programmers: they work with the audio personnel to create a realistic-sounding environment.

Tool Programmers: as previously mentioned, programmers often write software for artists, designers, and sound designers to use within the development studio.

AUDIO RELATED POSITIONS

High-quality music and sound effects are an integral part in any gaming project. This is also an area that many teams simply cannot afford to throw a great deal of money at. Having superb audio components like music, sound, and voice can greatly enhance the total experience for the consumer. The opposite is also true, however. Music that is done poorly can be keep people away from your product, regardless of its other qualities. The positions listed below are usually filled by key audio personnel, although sometimes a programmer or other team member will fill in as needed.

Musician

When compared with the stress and long hours of the programmers, musicians are often at the other end of the workload. They often have the least amount of work of any of the positions on the team. That's not to imply that they don't work hard; it's just that there isn't as much for them to do.

They usually are responsible only for the music for a game. While this is an important job, it doesn't typically take a great deal of time, as compared with the other team members' jobs. Because of the relatively short production times, musicians often have secondary work outside of the gaming industry.

Sound Effects

Depending on the makeup of a team, a musician could be involved with the creation of the sound effects in a game. This can often make up for the lack of work that they have and help to keep the budgets down. Another route that many teams choose to follow is the purchase of pre-existing sound effects. There are many sound effects companies that distribute their work on CD-ROMS or the Internet. Many teams choose to purchase the sounds produced by these companies and alter them to their liking.

ART RELATED POSITIONS

Artist

The artists are responsible for creating the graphics elements that make up a project. They often specialize in one area within a project, such as 3D graphics or 2D artwork such as textures. The artists usually work from a set of specifications given to them by the programmer. Unfortunately, artists and programmers often have many disagreements on these specifications. For instance, artists might want to increase the polygon counts on a 3D model so that their work will look better, while programmers may want to decrease these same counts to make the program run more smoothly.

Game artists have a variety of technical constraints imposed by the limitations of the hardware that they are creating for. Although hardware continues to increase in speed and go down in cost, there is never enough power to satisfy a development project. Therefore, it is often the artists who are given the responsibility to create objects that work within the constraints.

Depending on the development team, there are three basic types of artists.: character artists (or animators, as some prefer to be called), 3D modelers, and texture artists.

Character Artist

Character artists have one of the most demanding jobs on the team. They create all of the moveable objects in a game, such as the main character, a space ship or a vehicle. It is their job to turn the preliminary sketches that are often discussed by the entire team into a believable object on a computer screen.

Using 3D modeling tools like 3D Studio Max™, True-Space®, Maya® or Lightwave™, character artists use basic shapes and combine them to form characters. If you have never used a 3D-modeling program, you can think of it as a type of digital clay. Once created, characters are fleshed out with a 2D graphic image that is made in another program.

The character artists are also responsible for the animation of the objects. They may be required to animate a horse, a human being, or a creature that previously existed only in someone's mind. Character artists often look at real world examples to get their ideas on how a character should move. Depending on the type of game, they may have to create facial expressions or emotions, as well.

It's often the responsibility of a character artist to implement cut scenes in a game, as well. Many artists enjoy creating cut screens even more than creating the characters in the game. They have much greater freedom and are not restricted as to the number of polygons a certain object can have or the size of the object.

3D Modeler

The 3D modeler usually works on the settings in which a game takes place, such as a basketball arena or a Wild West wasteland. Background artists work hand-in-hand with the designer to create believable environments that work within the constraints of a game. Like character artists, they use a wide range of tools for their jobs, including both 2D and 3D graphics tools, although they usually only model static objects.

Texture Artist

Texture artists might be the best friend of the other artists. It is their job to take the work created by the modeler or character artist and add detail to it. For example, they could create a brick texture that, when added to a 3D box created by the modeler, creates the illusion of a pile of bricks. On the other hand, they could create a texture that looks like cheese, turning this same box into a block of cheese.

PRODUCER

A producer oversees the entire project and attempts to keep everything moving along as smoothly as possible. A producer often acts as an arbitrator to help patch up any problems between team members. For instance, if an artist wants to increase the color palette and a programmer wants to decrease it, the producer often makes the final decision on these types of key issues.

SECONDARY POSITIONS

There are several secondary positions that can be important to the development cycle, as well. Depending on the budget, these positions may or may not exist at all or could be filled by other members of the team.

Beta Tester

Beta testers test the playability of a game and look for bugs that may occur when the game is executed. This is one of the most undervalued of the positions and should never be done by the person responsible for programming the game. In reality, because of tight budgets and deadlines, beta testing is one of the steps that is often cut before it is completed, as due dates will unfortunately take precedence over most decisions. If adequate beta testing is performed, a development team can save a tremendous amount of time and resources without having to produce unnecessary patches at a later date.

Play Testers

The play testers are often confused with beta testers. The difference is that play testers only test the *playability* of a game. They often critique areas such as movement or graphic elements. Again, these positions are often filled by people who perform other tasks on the team. Unlike beta testers, play testers do not attempt to find or report bugs. Their purpose is to judge if a game is fun to play

Links to Game Programming Web Sites and Newsgroups

LINKS TO WEB SITES

Snok Game Project
http://tihlde.org/~torbjorv/snok/
A 3D-snake game, complete with source code.

Java Game Development Center
http://www.electricfunstuff.com/jgdc/
Java game development.

GameInstitute
http://www.gameinstitute.com/
Online game development courses!

Delphi Gamer / Development
http://www.savagesoftware.com.au/DelphiGamer/indexf.php
A site dedicated to Delphi game development.

Filipe's Page of Game Programming
http://www.mindlick.com/programming/
Various tutorials.

2D Game Programming
http://www.2dgame.nl/
Good 2D Site.

Damberg.de Game Programming
http://www.damberg.de/
A Visual Basic (VB) game programming site.

Lucky's VB Gaming Site
http://rookscape.com/vbgaming/
One of the best!

The Nexus
http://www.thenexus.bc.ca/
Another excellent VB site.

Amit's Game Programming Site

http://www-cs-students.stanford.edu/~amitp/gameprog.html
More information on path finding.

Game Developer's Conference

http://www.gdconf.com/
Home of the GDC – not much else to say.

Darwin3D GD Section

http://www.darwin3d.com/gamedev.htm
A collection of useful articles from *Game Developer Magazine.*

Java Game Development Center

http://www.electricfunstuff.com/jgdc/
Source code, theory, and other resources related to Java development.

Game Design Web Sites

http://www.cs.queensu.ca/~dalamb/Games/design/gameDesign Sites.
This is simply a collection of game development resources on the Internet.

Mr-GameMaker.Com

http://www.mr-gamemaker.co.uk/
Features tutorials on topics related to game development, including some fairly hard to find D3D information.

CFXWeb

http://cfxweb.planet-d.net/
A game programming and demo news site. It's updated quite often and features some good tutorials, links, and other related features. Definitely worth a look.

Golgotha Source Code

http://www.jitit.com/golgotha/

When Crack.Com went under, they released the source code to their project Golgotha. The entire game engine, art, and so on is available for download.

Gamasutra

http://www.gamasutra.com/

Gamasutra is *Game Developer Magazine's* Web site.

Mad Monkey

http://www.madmonkey.net

Mad Monkey focuses on the independent gaming scene. There you'll find information on projects currently in the works, programming tutorials, message forums, and plenty more.

Game Programming Megasite

http://www.perplexed.com/GPMega/index.htm

Tutorials and information.

Pawn's Game Programming Pages

http://www.aros.net/~npawn/

Rex Sound's Programming Engine.

The New Game Programmer's Guild

http://pages.vossnet.de/mgricken/newgpg/

Large Web ring for development sites.

GameProgrammer.Com

http://www.gameprogrammer.com/

Mostly old information.

GameDev.Net

http://www.gamedev.net

Articles, news, links, and more.

Game Development Search Engine
http://www.game-developer.com/
Search engine for game developers.

Linux Game Development Center
http://sunsite.auc.dk/linuxgames/
As the name says, mostly Linux materials.

flipCode
http://www.flipcode.com
Another highly recommended site!

NEWSGROUPS

Language Groups

comp.lang.asm.x86
x86 assembly language.

comp.lang.c
The C programming language.

comp.lang.c.moderated
Not much traffic, but good.

microsoft.public.vb
VB language.

microsoft.public.vb
VB language and DirectX.

microsoft.public.vb.winapi.graphics
Graphics and VB.

borland.public.delphi
Delphi Language.

borland.public.delphi.graphics
Delphi graphics.

macromedia.director.lingo
Director information.

Graphics Groups

comp.graphics.algorithms
BSP trees to texture mapping.

AI Groups

comp.ai.games
This newsgroup has useful information.

Game Groups

rec.games.programmer
Probably the most popular general newsgroup.

rec.games.design
Designing games.

Game Maker Actions Reference

This section describes all the important actions supported by Game Maker. The actions that Game Maker can perform are grouped into categories and are selected by clicking on the appropriate tab in the Object properties window. Within each tab are subcategories that group similar actions. The actions are listed under their respective groups and described below.

ACTIONS IN THE MOVE TAB

The actions found in the Move tab are listed below. A complete description of each of the actions is also provided here.

- Start Moving in Direction
- Set Direction and Speed
- Move in the Direction of a Point
- Set Horizontal Speed
- Set Vertical Speed
- Set Gravity
- Reverse Horizontal Direction
- Reverse Vertical Direction
- Set the Friction
- Jump to Given Position
- Jump to Start Position
- Jump to Random Position
- Snap to Grid
- Wrap when Moving Outside
- Move to Contact Position
- Bounce Against Objects

Start Moving in Direction

Use this action to move the instance of an object in a particular direction. A dialog box titled Start Moving in a Direction opens when this action is dragged to the Active Actions window as shown in Figure D.1. There are four editable properties in this dialog box.

The first editable property consists of three radio buttons labeled Self, Other, and Object. This allows you to move the instance of the object you are working with or move to a different instance of some other object. Choosing the radio button labeled Object results in the creation of a new text box as shown in Figure D.2. This allows you to choose the object to which you want to apply the current action.

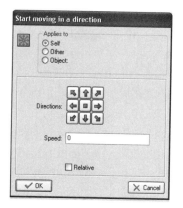

FIGURE D.1   Start Moving in a Direction Property box.

FIGURE D.2   Start Moving in a Direction with object Property box selected.

The next editable property defines the direction of motion. Images of eight arrows and a square are visible on this pop-up property window. Clicking the appropriate direction button defines the direction of motion of the instance of an object. For example, clicking on the left arrow button will make the instance move to the left. The square button in the center is used to stop the instance from moving. It is also possible to select multiple directions by clicking on multiple arrows. If multiple directions are selected, the game engine makes a random choice of direction. This provides the additional facility for moving instances of objects in random directions.

The next editable property defines the speed of the instance. The value is set in text box labeled Speed. In Game Maker, the speed is defined in pixels per step. The default value is 0. A value can be typed into the text box to define the speed with which the instance of the object moves.

The last editable property is the checkbox labeled Relative. An improper understanding of this property can result in objects moving at undesired speeds. When defining speed for objects, you have two choices. You can define the speed of the object relative to its prior speed or define the speed in absolute terms. If the speed is defined to be relative, the check mark on the Relative option needs to be enabled. In this case the new speed of the object is its old speed plus the speed defined in this property window. Typically the speed keeps increasing or decreasing depending on whether the speed was specified as a positive or negative value. To keep an object moving at a constant speed, it is best to uncheck the relative option and provide the absolute speed explicitly.

Set Direction and Speed

This action is used to set the direction of motion and speed of an object. This action provides more granular control while setting the direction of motion of the object. A dialog box titled Set Direction and Speed opens up when this action is dragged to the Active Actions window as shown in Figure D.3. There are four editable properties in this dialog box.

FIGURE D.3   Set Direction and Speed Property box.

As with the Start Moving in a Direction action, he first editable property consists of three radio buttons labeled Self, Other, and Object. This allows you to either move the instance of the object you are working with or move to a different instance of some other object. Choosing the radio button labeled Object results in the creation of a new text box as was shown in Figure D.2. This allows you to choose the object to which you would like to apply the current action.

The next editable property defines the direction of motion. Entering an angle that has a value between 0 and 360 degrees sets the direction of motion. An angle of 0 degrees defines motion to the right. An angle of 180 degrees defines motion to the left.

The next editable property defines the speed of the instance. The value is set in the text box labeled Speed. In Game Maker, speed is defined in pixels per step. The default value is 0. A value can be typed into the text box to define the speed at which the instance of the object moves.

As before, the last editable property is the checkbox labeled Relative. An improper understanding of this property can result in objects moving at undesired speeds. When defining speed for objects, you have two choices. You can define the speed of the object relative to its prior speed or in absolute terms. If the speed is defined to be relative, the check box on the Relative option needs to be selected. In this case the new speed of the object is its old speed plus the speed defined in this property window. Typically the speed keeps increasing or decreasing depending on whether the speed was specified as a positive or negative value. To keep an object moving at a constant speed, it is best to uncheck the Relative option and provide the absolute speed explicitly.

Move in the Direction of a Point

This action is used to set an object in motion by specifying a speed and the X and Y coordinates of a point toward which the object should move. This action provides a novel mechanism to control the object's direction of motion of the object and is described in detail in the following paragraphs. A dialog box titled Move in the Direction of a Point opens up when this action is dragged to the Active Actions window as shown in Figure D.4. There are five editable properties in this dialog box.

FIGURE D.4   Move in the Direction
of a Point Property box.

The first editable property consists of three radio buttons labeled Self, Other, and Object. This allows you to either move the instance of the object you are working with or move to a different instance of some other object. Choosing the radio button labeled Object results in the creation of a new text box as was shown in Figure D.2. This allows you to choose the object to which you would like to apply the current action.

The second and third editable properties define the X and Y coordinates of the position toward which the object should move. The absolute values of X and Y can be specified here or the X and Y coordinates of an object can be specified. Specifying absolute values for X and Y will make the object move toward the specified location. If ObjectA is to follow ObjectB, you can use this action in ObjectA to make this happen. The X value should be set to ObjectB.x and the Y value to ObjectB.y for ObjectA to follow ObjectB. If ObjectB moves, its X and Y coordinates would be reflected in its properties ObjectB.x and ObjectB.y, ObjectA would find its way toward ObjectB by using these two values. This action is also used if you want to create projectiles that lock in to a target.

The next editable property defines the speed of the instance. The value is set in the text box labeled Speed. In Game Maker, speed is defined in pixels per step. The default value is 0. A value can be typed into the text box to define the speed at which the instance of the object moves. The speed defined here is the absolute speed.

The last editable property is the checkbox labeled Relative. This field defines whether the location is an absolute location or a relative location. If the Relative box is checked, the position specified is relative to the current position of the instance. This check box applies only to position and not to the speed.

Set Horizontal Speed

This action is used to set an object in motion at a defined speed in the horizontal direction. A dialog box titled Set Horizontal Speed opens up when this action is dragged to the Active Actions window as shown in Figure D.5. There are three editable properties in this dialog box.

FIGURE D.5   Set Horizontal Speed Property box.

The first editable property consists of three radio buttons labeled Self, Other, and Object. This allows you to apply the current action to either the instance of the object you are working with or to a different instance of some other object. Choosing the radio button labeled Object results in the creation of a new text box as was shown in Figure D.2. This allows you to choose the object to which you would like to apply the current action.

The second property defines the horizontal speed of the object. A positive value moves the object to the right and a negative value moves it to the left. The vertical speed of the object remains unchanged when this action is used. If the object it to move diagonally, it needs both a horizontal and a vertical speed.

The last editable property is the checkbox labeled Relative. This field defines whether the speed is relative or absolute. If the Relative box is checked, the speed is augmented with the value provided. A positive value increases the speed and a negative value lowers the speed. If the Relative box is unchecked, the specified speed is directly applied to the object.

Set Vertical Speed

This action is used to set an object in motion at a defined speed in the vertical direction. A dialog box titled Set Vertical Speed opens up when this action is dragged to the Active Actions window as shown in Figure D.6. There are three editable properties in this dialog box.

FIGURE D.6 Set Vertical Speed Property box.

The first editable property consists of three radio buttons labeled Self, Other, and Object. This allows you to apply the current action to either the instance of the object you are working with or to a different instance of some other object. Choosing the radio button labeled Object results in the creation of a new text box as was shown in Figure D.2. This allows you to choose the object to which you would like to apply the current action.

The second property defines the vertical speed of the object. A positive value moves the object down and a negative value moves it up. The horizontal speed of the object remains unchanged when this action is used. If the object is to move diagonally, it needs both a horizontal and a vertical speed.

The last editable property is the checkbox labeled Relative. This field defines whether the speed is relative or absolute. If the Relative box is checked, the speed is augmented with the value provided. A positive value increases the speed and a negative value lowers the speed. If the Relative box is unchecked, the specified speed is directly applied to the object.

Set Gravity

This action is used to simulate the effect of a gravitational force on objects. Unlike real gravity, this action can set the strength of the gravitational force and its direction to values of our choice. A dialog box titled Set Gravity opens up when this action is dragged to the Active Actions window as shown in Figure D.7. There are four editable properties in this dialog box.

FIGURE D.7   Set Gravity
Property box.

The first editable property consists of three radio buttons labeled Self, Other, and Object. This allows you to apply the current action to either the instance of the object you are working with or to a different instance of some other object. Choosing the radio button labeled Object results in the creation of a new text box as was shown in Figure D.2. This allows you to choose the object to which you would like to apply the current action.

The second property defines the vertical speed of the object. A positive value moves the object down and a negative value moves it up. The horizontal speed of the object remains unchanged when this action is used. If the object is to move diagonally, it needs both a horizontal and a vertical speed.

The next editable property (direction) defines the direction of the gravitational field. An angle of 0 degrees defines a gravitational field to the right. An angle of 180 degrees defines a field to the left. Entering a value that has any value between 0 and 360 degrees can create any other directional field. Specifying a value of 270 degrees for this field creates a gravitational field toward the bottom of the screen.

The last editable field defines the magnitude of the gravitational field. In the real world, the speed of an object falling in a gravitational field steadily increases. In Game Maker, this effect is simulated by specifying the speed with which the object accelerates on every cycle of the game. A very small value of 0.01 specified in this field along with a directional value of 270 provides a realistic gravitational effect. If the Relative box is checked, the speed and the direction change in increments by the specified values on every cycle of the game.

Reverse Horizontal Direction

This action is used to reverse the direction of horizontal motion of the object. This can, for example, be used when you want to implement your own custom behavior to bounce objects off obstacles. A dialog box titled Reverse Horizontal Direction opens up when this action is dragged to the Active Actions window as shown in Figure D.9. There is one editable property in this dialog box.

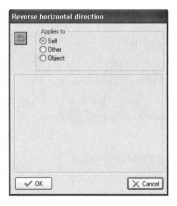

FIGURE D.8   Reverse Horizontal
Direction Property box.

The editable property consists of three radio buttons labeled Self, Other, and Object. This allows you to apply the current action to either the instance of the object you are working with or to a different instance of some other object. Choosing the radio button labeled Object results in the creation of a new text box as was shown in Figure D.2. This allows you to choose the object to which you would like to apply the current action.

Reverse Vertical Direction

This action is used to reverse the direction of vertical motion of the object. This can, for example, be used when you want to implement your own custom behavior to bounce objects off obstacles. A dialog box titled Reverse Vertical Direction opens up when this action is dragged to the Active Actions window as shown in Figure D.9. There is one editable property in this dialog box.

The editable property consists of three radio buttons labeled Self, Other, and Object. This allows you to apply the current action to either the instance of the object you are working with or to a different instance of some other object. Choosing the radio button labeled Object results in the creation of a new text box as was shown in Figure D.2. This allows you to choose the object to which you would like to apply the current action.

Set the Friction

This action defines the frictional component that slows down objects that are in motion. A dialog box titled Set the Friction opens up when this action is dragged to the Active Actions window as shown in Figure D.10. There are two editable properties in this dialog box.

FIGURE D.9   Reverse Vertical Direction Property box.

FIGURE D.10   Set the Friction Property box.

The first editable property consists of three radio buttons labeled Self, Other, and Object. This allows you to apply the current action to either the instance of the object you are working with or to a different instance of some other object. Choosing the radio button labeled Object results in the creation of a new text box as was shown in Figure D.2. This allows you to choose the object to which you would like to apply the current action.

The next editable property defines the frictional component. The value specified here is used to decrementally change the speed of the object on every cycle. A typical value of 0.01 reduces the speed of the object by 0.01 on every game engine cycle. The frictional value is applied to reduce the speed until the speed becomes 0. Higher values here would bring the object to rest much faster.

Jump to Given Position

This action is used to move the instance of an object to a specified position of the game room. A dialog box titled Jump to a Given Position opens up when this action is dragged to the Active Actions window as shown in Figure D.11. There are four editable properties in this dialog box.

FIGURE D.11   Jump to a Given Position Property box.

The first editable property consists of three radio buttons labeled Self, Other, and Object. This allows you to apply the current action to either the instance of the object you are working with or to a different instance of some other object. Choosing the radio button labeled Object results in the creation of a new text box as was shown in Figure D.2. This allows you to choose the object to which you would like to apply the current action.

The second and third editable properties define the X and Y coordinates the object should jump to. These two values together with the Relative checkbox define the final location of the object.

The last editable property is the checkbox labeled Relative. This field defines whether the final location is relative to the current location or is an absolute location. If the Relative box is checked, the object jumps to a position that is X and Y units away from its current location. The object can be moved diagonally by specifying a relative value for the X and Y value. If the Relative box is unchecked, the object jumps to the absolute location specified.

Jump to Start Position

This action is used to move the instance of an object to its starting position. A dialog box titled Jump to Start Position opens up when this action is dragged to the Active Actions window as shown in Figure D.12. There is one editable property in this dialog box.

FIGURE D.12   Jump to Start Position Property box.

The editable property consists of three radio buttons labeled Self, Other, and Object. This allows you to apply the current action to either the instance of the object you are working with or to a different instance of some other object. Choosing the radio button labeled Object results in the creation of a new text box as was shown in Figure D.2. This allows you to choose the object to which you would like to apply the current action.

Jump to Random Position

This action is used to move the instance to a random position within the game room. The position is chosen such that it does not sit on top of any other instance of a solid object. A dialog box titled Jump to a Random Position opens up when this action is dragged to the Active Actions window as shown in Figure D.13. There are three editable properties in this dialog box.

The first editable property consists of three radio buttons labeled Self, Other, and Object. This allows you to apply the current action to either the instance of the object you are working with or to a different instance of some other object. Choosing the radio button labeled Object results in the creation of a new text box as was shown in Figure D.2. This allows you to choose the object to which you would like to apply the current action.

The second and third properties define the X and Y snapping values. The final coordinates the object will jump to will be an integer multiple of the indicated value.

Snap to Grid

This action is used to align the position of an instance of an object on a grid. A dialog box titled Snap to Grid opens up when this action is dragged to the Active Actions window as shown in Figure D.14. There are three editable properties in this dialog box.

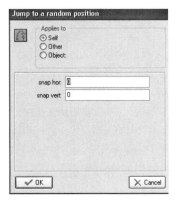

FIGURE D.13   Jump to a Random Position Property box.

FIGURE D.14   Snap to Grid Property box.

The first editable property consists of three radio buttons labeled Self, Other, and Object. This allows you to apply the current action to either the instance of the object you are working with or to a different instance of some other object. Choosing the radio button labeled Object results in the creation of a new text box as was shown in Figure D.2. This allows you to choose the object to which you would like to apply the current action.

The second and third properties define the X and Y values for the size of the grid. The instance of the object will be aligned to snap to a grid defined by these two values.

Wrap When Moving Outside

This action is used to make an instance of a moving object wrap around the edge of a room. This enables the object to appear on the other side of the room when it leaves the opposite side. A dialog box titled Wrap When Moving Outside opens up when this action is dragged to the Active Actions window as shown in Figure D.15. There are three editable properties in this dialog box.

FIGURE D.15   Wrap When
Moving Outside Property box.

The first editable property consists of three radio buttons labeled Self, Other, and Object. This allows you to apply the current action to either the instance of the object you are working with or to a different instance of some other object. Choosing the radio button labeled Object results in the creation of a new text box as was shown in Figure D.2. This allows you to choose the object to which you would like to apply the current action.

The second editable property defines the wrapping direction. It can be vertical, horizontal, or both. Setting the vertical wrapping option enables the object to reenter the room when it exits through the upper or lower boundaries of the room. Setting the horizontal wrapping option enables the object to reenter the room when it exits through the left or right boundaries of the room. Both horizontal and vertical options can be set so that the object reenters the room when it exits through any of the room boundaries. This action is normally used in conjunction with an Outside Room event.

Move to Contact Position

This action is used to move an instance of an object in a specific direction until it comes in contact with another object. The contact position is defined as the position of an object just before it collides with another object. If the object is already colliding with another object, it does not move. A dialog box titled Move to Contact Position opens up when this action is dragged to the Active Actions window as shown in Figure D.16. There are four editable properties in this dialog box.

FIGURE D.16 Move to Contact Position Property box.

The first editable property consists of three radio buttons labeled Self, Other, and Object. This allows you to apply the current action to either the instance of the object you are working with or to a different instance of some other object. Choosing the radio button labeled Object results in the creation of a new text box as was shown in Figure D.2. This allows you to choose the object to which you would like to apply the current action.

The next editable property, direction, defines the direction of motion. Entering an angle that has any value between 0 and 360 degrees sets the direction of motion. An angle of 0 degrees defines motion to the right. An angle of 180 degrees defines motion to the left.

The next editable property, maximum, defines the maximum distance the object should be allowed to travel before its reaches a contact position.

The last editable property, against, defines whether the contact position could be solid objects only or all kinds of objects.

Bounce Against Objects

This action is used to bounce a moving object off another object when a collision occurs. A dialog box titled Bounce Against Objects opens up when this action is dragged to the Active Actions window as shown in Figure D.17. There are three editable properties in this dialog box.

The first editable property consists of three radio buttons labeled Self, Other, and Object. This allows you to apply the current action to either the instance of the object you are working with or to a different instance of some other object. Choosing the radio button labeled Object results in the creation of a new text box as was shown in Figure D.2. This allows you to choose the object to which you would like to apply the current action.

The second editable property, precise, defines whether you prefer an accurate bouncing mechanism for all cases.

FIGURE D.17   Bounce Against Objects Property box.

Setting this value to false bounces objects correctly in the horizontal and vertical directions alone. Setting this value to true enables accurate bouncing of objects off slanted and curved walls.

The third editable property, against, defines whether the object should bounce of solid objects or all objects.

ACTIONS IN THE MAIN1 TAB

The actions under found in the Main1 tab are listed below. A complete description of each of the actions is also provided here.

- Create an Instance of an Object
- Create an Instance of an Object with Motion
- Create Instance of Random Object
- Create Instance of Random Object
- Change the Instance
- Destroy the Instance
- Destroy Instance at a Position
- Change the Sprite
- Transform the Sprite
- Set Sprite Blending
- Play a Sound
- Stop a Sound

- If a Sound Is Playing
- Go to Previous Room
- Go to Next Room
- Restart the Current Room
- Go to a Different Room
- If Previous Room Exists
- If Next Room Exists

Create an Instance of an Object

In a dynamic game, this action is used frequently to create new instance of all kinds of objects. A Create event is received by the newly created objects as a result of this action. A dialog box titled Create an Instance of an Object opens up when this action is dragged to the Active Actions window as shown in Figure D.18. There are five editable properties in this dialog box.

FIGURE D.18   Create an Instance of an Object Property box.

The first editable property consists of three radio buttons labeled Self, Other, and Object. This allows you to apply the current action to either the instance of the object you are working with or to a different instance of some other object. Choosing the radio button labeled Object results in the creation of a new text box as was shown in Figure D.2. This allows you to choose the object to which you would like to apply the current action.

The second editable property, object, defines the type of object that would be created. A drop-down list shows all the objects that could be created.

The next two editable properties define the X and Y coordinates of the position at which the object should be created. The values specified here are either absolute values or relative values depending on the whether the relative box is checked.

The last editable property is the checkbox labeled Relative. This field defines whether the final location is relative to the current location or is an absolute location. If the Relative box is checked, the new object is created at a distance of X and Y units relative to its current location. If the Relative box is unchecked, the object is created at the specified absolute location.

Create an Instance of an Object with Motion

This action is used to create a new instance of an object and set it in motion. A Create event is received by the newly created objects as a result of this action. A dialog box titled Create an Instance of an Object with a Motion opens up when this action is dragged to the Active Actions window as shown in Figure D.19. There are seven editable properties in this dialog box.

FIGURE D.19 Create an Instance of an Object with a Motion Property box.

The first editable property consists of three radio buttons labeled Self, Other, and Object. This allows you to apply the current action to either the instance of the object you are working with or to a different instance of some other object. Choosing the radio button labeled Object results in the creation of a new text box as was shown in Figure D.2. This allows you to choose the object to which you would like to apply the current action.

The second editable property, object, defines the type of object that would be created. A drop-down list shows all the objects that could be created.

The next two editable properties define the X and Y coordinates of the position at which the object should be created. The values specified here are either absolute values or relative values depending on the whether the relative box is checked.

The next editable property defines the speed of the instance. The value is set in the text box labeled Speed. In Game Maker, speed is defined in pixels per step. The default value is 0. A value can be typed in into the text box to define the speed at which the instance of the object moves.

The next editable property defines the direction of motion. Entering an angle that has any value between 0 and 360 degrees sets the direction of motion. An angle of 0 degrees defines motion to the right. An angle of 180 degrees defines motion to the left. If you want the newly created instance to move in the same direction as the object that created it, you can type in the value Direction in this field. Every object has a property called direction that defines the direction it travels when it is set in motion.

The last editable property is the checkbox labeled Relative. This field defines whether the final location is relative to the current location or is an absolute location. If the Relative box is checked, the new object is created at a distance of X and Y units relative to its current location. Note that this check box does not apply to the speed and direction properties. If the Relative box is unchecked, the object is created at the specified absolute location.

Create Instance of Random Object

This action is used to randomly create an instance of an object from a selection of up to four objects. This action can be used to provide the player with an element of surprise, since it the objects are randomly chosen and created from the predefined list. A dialog box titled Create an Instance of Random Object opens up when this action is dragged to the Active Actions window as was shown in Figure D.20. There are eight editable properties in this dialog box.

FIGURE D.20   Create an Instance of Random Object Property box.

The first editable property consists of three radio buttons labeled Self, Other, and Object. This allows you to apply the current action to either the instance of the object you are working with or to a different instance of some other object. Choosing the radio button labeled Object results in the creation of a new text box as was shown in Figure D.2. This allows you to choose the object to which you would like to apply the current action.

The next four editable properties, object1, object2, object3, and object4 provide a mechanism with which to choose four different objects. The default value for these fields is No object. You need to specify at least one of these objects to refer to a real object.

The next two fields define the X and Y coordinates at which the object should be created. These two values together with the Relative checkbox define the final location of the created object.

The last editable property is the checkbox labeled Relative. This field defines whether the final location is relative to the current location or is an absolute location. If the Relative box is checked, the new object is created at a distance of X and Y units away from the original object's current location. If the Relative box is unchecked, the object is created at the specified absolute location.

Change the Instance

This action is used to change the current instance of an object into an instance of different object. An instance of a seed object could be converted into a plant object after a defined time interval, for example. A dialog box titled Change the Instance opens up when this action is dragged to the Active Actions window as was shown in Figure D.21. There are three editable properties in this dialog box.

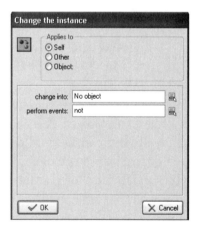

FIGURE D.21   Change the Instance
Property box.

The first editable property consists of three radio buttons labeled Self, Other, and Object. This allows you to apply the current action to either the instance of the object you are working with or to a different instance of some other object. Choosing the radio button labeled Object results in the creation of a new text box as was shown in Figure D.2. This allows you to choose the object to which you would like to apply the current action.

The second editable property, change into, defines the instance type into which the current object will be transformed.

The third editable property defines whether or not the Destroy event for the current object and the Create event for the new object need to be performed.

Destroy the Instance

This action is used to destroy the instance. A dialog box titled Destroy the Instance opens up when this action is dragged to the Active Actions window as shown in Figure D.22. Only one property needs to be defined in this dialog box.

The only editable property consists of three radio buttons labeled Self, Other, and Object. This allows you to apply the current action to either the instance of the object you are working with or to a different instance of some other object. Choosing the radio button labeled Object results in the creation of a new text box as was shown in Figure D.2. This allows you to choose the object you would like to destroy.

Destroy Instance at a Position

This action is used to destroy all instances whose bounding box encompasses a given point. A dialog box titled Destroy Instance at a Position opens up when this action is dragged to the Active Actions window as shown in Figure D.23. Four properties need to be defined in this dialog box.

The first editable property consists of three radio buttons labeled Self, Other, and Object. This allows you to apply the current action to either the instance of the object you are working with or to a different instance of some other object. Choosing the radio button labeled Object results in the creation of a new text box as was shown in Figure D.2. This allows

FIGURE D.22 Destroy the Instance Property box.

FIGURE D.23 Destroy Instance at a Position Property box.

you to choose the object to which you would like to apply the current action.

The next two editable fields define the X and Y coordinates for the point.

The last editable property is the checkbox labeled Relative. This field defines whether the location of the point is relative to the current location or is an absolute location. If the Relative box is checked, objects whose boundary boxes are at a distance of X and Y units from the object's current location are destroyed. If the Relative box is unchecked, the object whose boundary box encompasses the specified absolute location is destroyed.

Change the Sprite

This action is used to replace the sprite of an instance of an object. A dialog box titled Change the Instance opens up when this action is dragged to the Active Actions window as shown in Figure D.24. Four properties need to be defined in this dialog box.

The first editable property consists of three radio buttons labeled Self, Other, and Object. This allows you to apply the current action to either the instance of the object you are working with or to a different instance of some other object.

FIGURE D.24   Change the Instance Property box.

Choosing the radio button labeled Object results in the creation of a new text box as was shown in Figure D.2. This allows you to choose the object to which you would like to apply the current action.

The second editable property, sprite, defines the name of the new sprite to be used in this action.

The third editable property, sub image, defines the index into the sprite array if the sprite is animated. The normal value would be 0 if there was no animation. A value of −1 displays the current image. Keep in mind that animated sprites consist of a series of sprites displayed one after the other, and this is where the index comes into play.

The last editable property, speed, defines the rate at which the sprites are replaced. A value of 1 displays all sprites sequentially. A speed of 0 displays only one sprite and does not show any animation. If the value is larger than 1, subimages are skipped during the display process.

Destroy the Instance

This action is used to destroy the sprite of an instance of an object. A dialog box titled Destroy the Instance opens up when this action is dragged to the Active Actions window as shown in Figure D.25. Three properties need to be defined in this dialog box.

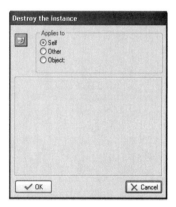

FIGURE D.25   Destroy the
Instance Property box.

The editable property consists of three radio buttons labeled Self, Other, and Object. This allows you to apply the current action to either the instance of the object you are working with or to a different instance of some other object. Choosing the radio button labeled Object results in the creation of a new text box as was shown in Figure D.2. This allows you to choose the object to which you would like to apply the current action.

Destroy Instances at a Position

This action is used to destroy the instances of an object at a given X, Y position. A dialog box titled Destroy Instances at a Position opens up when this action is dragged to the Active Actions window as shown in Figure D.26.

Transform the Sprite

This action is only available in the registered version of Game Maker. It is used to rotate, scale, and flip the sprite.

Set Sprite Blending

This action is only available in the registered version of Game Maker. It is used to change to color of the sprite by blending it with other colors.

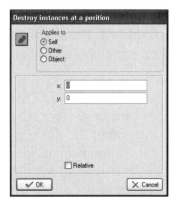

FIGURE D.26 Destroy Instances at a Position Property box.

Play a Sound

This action is used to play a sound file that has been loaded as a resource. WAV files MIDI files can be used. The computer synthesizes music from MIDI files, so if a Midi file is played, the previous Midi file is stopped. WAV files can be played together. A dialog box titled Play a Sound opens up when this action is dragged to the active actions window as shown in Figure D.27. Two properties need to be defined in this dialog box.

FIGURE D.27 Play a Sound Property box.

The first editable property defines the sound resource that has to be played. The second editable property allows for playing the music continuously or just once.

Stop a Sound

This action is used to stop the selected sound. If multiple instances of this sound are playing, all are stopped. A dialog box titled Stop a Sound opens up when this action is dragged to the Active Actions window as shown in Figure D.28. One property needs to be defined in this dialog box.

The only editable property that needs to be set for this action is to define the sound resource that has to be stopped.

If a Sound Is Playing

This action is a decision-making action block. It checks to see if a particular sound resource is playing or not and takes the appropriate action. If the sound resource is playing, the next sequential action is performed. Otherwise it is skipped. A dialog box titled If a Sound Is Playing opens up when this action is dragged to the Active Actions window as shown in Figure D.29. One property needs to be defined in this dialog box.

FIGURE D.28   Stop a Sound Property box.

FIGURE D.29   If a Sound Is Playing Property box.

The editable property that needs to be set for this action block is to define the sound resource that has to be checked.

Go to Previous Room

This action is used to move to the previous room in the game. A dialog box titled Go to Previous Room opens up when this action is dragged to the Active Actions window as shown in Figure D.30. One property needs to be defined in this dialog box.

The editable property that needs to be set defines the graphical effects that take place when the room transition occurs. The default transition provides no graphical effects.

FIGURE D.30   Go to Previous Room Property box.

Go to Next Room

This action is used to move to the next room in the game. A dialog box titled Go to Next Room opens up when this action is dragged to the Active Actions window as shown in Figure D.31. One property needs to be defined in this dialog box.

The editable property that needs to be set defines the graphical effects that take place when the room transition occurs. The default transition provides no graphical effects.

Restart the Current Room

This action is used to reload and restart the current room in the game. A dialog box titled Restart the Current Room opens up when this action is dragged to the Active Actions window as shown in Figure D.32. One property needs to be defined in this dialog box.

FIGURE D.31   Go to Next Room Property box.

FIGURE D.32   Restart the Current Room Property box.

The editable property that needs to be set defines the graphical effects that take place when the room transition occurs. The default transition provides no graphical effects.

Go to a Different Room

This action is used to transition to a specific room in the game. A dialog box titled Go to a Different Room opens up when this action is dragged to the Active Actions window as shown in Figure D.33. Two properties need to be defined in this dialog box.

The first editable property that needs to be set defines the name of the room to transition to. You are allowed to choose from any of the available rooms that have been created in the game.

FIGURE D.33   Go to a Different
Room Property box.

The second editable property that needs to be set defines
the graphical effects that take place when the room transition
occurs. The default transition provides no graphical effects.

If Previous Room Exists

This action is a decision-making action block. It checks to see
if a previous room exists and takes the appropriate action. If
the previous room exists, the next sequential action is performed. Otherwise the next action is skipped.

If Next Room Exists

This action is a decision-making action block. It checks to see
if a next room exists and takes the appropriate action. If the
next room exists, the next sequential action is performed.
Otherwise it is skipped.

ACTIONS IN THE MAIN2 TAB

The actions under found in the Main2 tab are listed below. A
complete description of each of the actions is also provided
here.

- Set an Alarm Clock
- Sleep for a While
- Display a Message
- Show Game Info
- Restart the Game
- End the Game
- Save the Game
- Load the Game
- Set Alarm Clock

Set Alarm Clock

This action is used to create software alarm clocks. Each instance can use up to 12 alarm clocks. The alarm clock is set by defining the number of steps that need to elapse before an Alarm event is triggered. A dialog box titled Set an Alarm Clock opens up when this action is dragged to the Active Actions window as shown in Figure D.34. Four properties need to be defined in this dialog box.

FIGURE D.34   Set an Alarm Clock Property box.

The first editable property consists of three radio buttons labeled Self, Other, and Object. This allows you to apply the current action to either the instance of the object you are working with or to a different instance of some other object. Choosing the radio button labeled Object results in the creation of a new text box as was shown in Figure D.2. This allows you to choose the object to which you would like to apply the current action.

The second editable property, number of steps, defines the duration to wait before triggering an Alarm event. The duration is defined using the appropriate quantity of steps. One second takes approximately 30 steps. If the Alarm event has to be generated after 2 seconds, this editable box has to be filled with a value of 60. If the value is less than or equal to zero, the alarm is turned off.

The third editable box defines the alarm clock you intend to use. You could choose from the list of alarms.

The last editable property is the checkbox labeled Relative. This field defines whether the delay for the alarm changes incrementally or decrementally from its previous value or if the value provided is an absolute value. If the relative box is checked, the value provided in the Number of Steps field is added to the old value to define a new delay. If the Relative box is unchecked, the value provided in the Number of Steps field is used as an absolute value for the delay.

Sleep for a While

This action is used to provide a delay to accomplish some task. It could be typically used to provide a delay for the user to read the screen before moving on to the next room. A dialog box titled Sleep for a While opens up when this action is dragged to the Active Actions window as shown in Figure D.35. Two properties need to be defined in this dialog box.

The first editable property, milliseconds, defines the desired delay in milliseconds.

The second editable property, redraw, is used to indicate if the screen has to be redrawn or not at the end of the sleep period.

Display a Message

This action is used to display a message to the user. The message appears in a message box and the user has to click the

OK button to dismiss the message. A dialog box titled Display a Message opens up when this action is dragged to the Active Actions window as shown in Figure D.36. One property needs to be defined in this dialog box.

FIGURE D.35   Sleep for a While Property box.

FIGURE D.36   Display a Message Property box.

The editable property that needs to be defined is labeled Message in the dialog box. This is where the message has to be typed in. The # symbol is used for new line characters, and expressions are embedded inside single or double quotes. If you require the # symbol itself in your message, use the escape sequence \# to display it.

Show Game Info

This action is used to display the game information window.

Restart the Game

This action is used to restart the game.

End the Game

This action is used to end the game.

Save the Game

This action is used to save the game. A dialog box titled Save the Game opens up when this action is dragged to the Active Actions window as shown in Figure D.37. One property needs to be defined in this dialog box.

The editable property that needs to be defined is labeled filename in the dialog box. The name of the file that would hold the saved data needs to be provided here.

Load the Game

This action is used to load a game from a file. A dialog box titled Load the Game opens up when this action is dragged to the Active Actions window as shown in Figure D.38. One property needs to be defined in this dialog box.

FIGURE D.37 Save the Game Property box.

FIGURE D.38 Load the Game Property box.

The editable property that needs to be defined is labeled filename in the dialog box. The name of the file that holds the saved data needs to be provided here.

ACTIONS IN THE CONTROL TAB

The actions found in the Control tab are listed below. A complete description of each of the actions is also provided here.

- If Position Is Collision Free
- If There Is a Collision at a Position
- If There Is an Object at a Position
- If the Number of Instance is a Value
- With a Chance Perform Next Action
- If the User Answers Yes to a Question
- If an Expression Is True
- If a Mouse Button is Pressed
- If Instance Is Aligned on a Grid
- Start of Block and End of Block
- Else
- Exit this Event
- Repeat Next Action
- Execute a Piece of Code
- Put Some Comment
- Set the Value of a Variable
- If a Variable Has a Value
- Draw the Value of a Variable

If Position Is Collision Free

This action block checks to see if a location is devoid of objects. This action is typically used to check whether an instance can move to a particular position within the game room. The answer to this is either true or false. The next action is executed if the result is true and there are no objects that collide with the current object at the specified location. A dialog box titled If a Position Is Collision Free opens up when this action is dragged to the Active Actions window as shown in Figure D.39. Six properties need to be defined in this dialog box.

The first editable property consists of three radio buttons labeled Self, Other, and Object. This allows you to apply the current action to either the instance of the object you are working with or to a different instance of some other object. Choosing the radio button labeled Object results in the cre-

FIGURE D.39 If a Position Is
Collision Free Property box.

ation of a new text box as was shown in Figure D.2. This
allows you to choose the object to which you would like to
apply the current action.

The second and third editable properties are labeled X
and Y. The values provided here define the location where
the presence of a colliding object is searched.

The fourth editable property is labeled objects. The value
provided here defines whether the colliding object can be a
solid object or any object.

The fifth editable property is a checkbox labeled Relative.
If it is checked, the X and Y values are treated as relative coordinates; otherwise they are taken as absolute coordinates.

The sixth editable property is a checkbox labeled Not. It
negates the logic used by this action block and executes the
next action block only if the result is false.

If There Is a Collision at a Position

This action block checks to see if a location is occupied by any
object. This action is typically used to check whether an instance can move to a particular position within the game
room. The answer to this is either true or false. The next action
is executed if the result is true and there are objects that collide
with the current object at the specified location. A dialog box

titled If There Is a Collision at a Position opens up when this action is dragged to the Active Actions window as shown in Figure D.40. Six properties need to be defined in this dialog box.

FIGURE D.40   If there Is a Collision at a Position Property box.

The first editable property consists of three radio buttons are labeled Self, Other, and Object. This allows you to apply the current action to either the instance of the object you are working with or to a different instance of some other object. Choosing the radio button labeled Object results in the creation of a new text box as was shown in Figure D.2. This allows you to choose the object to which you would like to apply the current action.

The second and third editable properties are labeled X and Y. The values provided here define the location where the presence of a colliding object is searched.

The fourth editable property is labeled objects. The value provided here defines whether the colliding object can be a solid object or any object.

The fifth editable property is a checkbox labeled Relative. If it is checked, the X and Y values are treated as relative coordinates; otherwise they are taken as absolute coordinates.

The sixth editable property is a checkbox labeled Not. It negates the logic used by this action block and executes the next action block only if the result is false.

If There Is an Object at a Position

This action block checks to see if a location is occupied by a specific object. The answer to this is either true or false. The next action is executed if the result is true. A dialog box titled If There Is an Object at a Position opens up when this action is dragged to the Active Actions window as shown in Figure D.41. Six properties need to be defined in this dialog box.

FIGURE D.41   If there is an Object at a Position Property box.

The first editable property consists of three radio buttons labeled Self, Other, and Object. This allows you to apply the current action to either the instance of the object you are working with or to a different instance of some other object. Choosing the radio button labeled Object results in the creation of a new text box as was shown in Figure D.2. This allows you to choose the object to which you would like to apply the current action.

The second editable property is labeled object. The value provided here defines the type of object we are looking for.

The third and fourth editable properties are labeled X and Y. The values provided here define the location where the presence of a colliding object is searched.

The fifth editable property is a checkbox labeled Relative. If it is checked, the X and Y values are treated as relative co-ordinates; otherwise they are taken as absolute coordinates.

The sixth editable property is a checkbox labeled Not. It negates the logic used by this action block and executes the next action block only if the result is false.

If the Number of Instance Is a Value

This action is used to check the instance count of a specific kind of object. If the current count of instances of the object is equal to (or greater than or smaller than) the number provided, the next action is executed. A dialog box titled If the Number of Instances Is a Value opens up when this action is dragged to the Active Actions window as shown in Figure D.42. Four properties need to be defined in this dialog box.

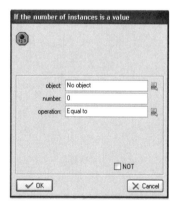

FIGURE D.42   If the Number of Instances is a Value Property box.

The first editable property consists of three radio buttons labeled Self, Other, and Object. This allows you to apply the current action to either the instance of the object you are working with or to a different instance of some other object.

Choosing the radio button labeled Object results in the creation of a new text box as was shown in Figure D.2. This allows you to choose the object to which you would like to apply the current action.

The second editable property, object, defines the type of object that is being counted.

The third editable property, number, defines the number of instances we are looking for.

The fourth editable property, operation, defines the logical operation to be performed. It could be equal to, greater than, or smaller than.

With a Chance Perform Next Action

This action simulates the throwing of a die. If the result is one, the next action is executed. As the number of sides of the die is increased, the chances of getting a one get reduced. A dialog box titled With a Chance Perform Next Action opens up when this action is dragged to the Active Actions window as shown in Figure D.43. Two properties that need to be defined in this dialog box.

The first editable property defines the number of sides for the die.

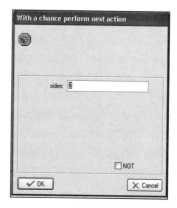

FIGURE D.43   With a Chance Perform Next Action Property box.

The second editable property is a checkbox labeled Not. It negates the logic used by this action block and executes the next action block only if the result is false.

If the User Answers Yes to a Question

This action block presents the user with a dialog box that contains a question, a Yes button, and a No button. The action that follows is executed if the user presses the Yes button. A dialog box titled If the User Answers Yes to a Question opens up when this action is dragged to the Active Actions window as shown in Figure D.44. Two properties need to be defined in this dialog box.

The first editable property, question, provides space for typing in the question that would be presented to the user.

The second editable property is a checkbox labeled Not. It negates the logic used by this action block and executes the next action block only if the result is false.

If an Expression Is True

This action block is the same as the above action block except that the user provides an expression instead of a question. If the result of the evaluation is true, the next action is executed.

If a Mouse Button Is Pressed

This action is used to take appropriate action based on the mouse button clicked. If the mouse button specified by the user is clicked, the next action is executed. A dialog box titled If a Mouse Button Is Pressed opens up when this action is dragged to the Active Actions window as shown in Figure D.45. One property needs to be defined in this dialog box.

The editable property labeled button provides a drop-down list of choices the user can select from.

If Instance Is Aligned on a Grid

This action is used to make an appropriate decision based on the absence or presence of an object on a specified grid within the game room. If the object is aligned with the grid, the next

FIGURE D.44   If the user answers yes to a question Property box.

FIGURE D.45   If a Mouse Button is Pressed Property box.

action is performed. If not, it is skipped. A dialog box titled If Instance Is Aligned on a Grid opens up when this action is dragged to the Active Actions window as shown in Figure D.46. Three properties need to be defined in this dialog box.

The first two editable properties, snap hor and snap ver, enable the user to provide the horizontal and vertical spacing for the grid. A decision is made as to whether the object aligns on this grid.

The second editable property is a checkbox labeled Not. It negates the logic used by this action block and executes the next action block only if the result is false.

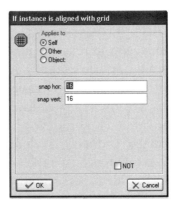

FIGURE D.46   If Instance is Aligned on a Grid Property box.

Start of Block and End of Block

The Start of Block action block delineates the beginning of a sequence of action blocks that form a group. The End of Block action block delineates the end of the sequence of blocks. The action blocks that lie between a start and end block can be thought of as a single entity that either gets executed together or never gets executed at all. This is useful when multiple actions need to be performed when a certain condition is true.

Else

The Else action block is used for situations where a set of actions needs to be executed when a condition is not satisfied. Most of the actions blocks that check for a condition execute a set of blocks if the result is true. Adding an Else block at the end facilitates the execution of a set of action blocks when the condition is false.

Exit this Event

This action is used to stop the execution of all the other actions for a particular event. There may be a list of a series of actions to execute when a certain event occurs. Of these events, a subset may need to be executed when a certain condition is satisfied. The Exit this Event action can be used here to prematurely abort the normal sequence of execution.

Repeat Next Action

This action is used to repeat the next action or block of actions a certain number of times. A dialog box titled Repeat Next Action opens up when this action is dragged to the Active Actions window as shown in Figure D.47. One property needs to be defined in this dialog box.

The editable property labeled times allows the user to enter a count that represents the number of times the action that follows this block is executed.

FIGURE D.47   Repeat Next
Action Property box.

Execute a Piece of Code

Game Maker allows the use of scripts to define complex actions. Scripts provide more control over the objects involved in those actions. This action allows the user to create and execute code. An editor window titled Execute a Piece of Code opens up when this action is dragged to the Active Actions window as shown in Figure D.48. The code (script) has to be typed into this window and then saved by clicking the green checkbox on the upper-left corner of this window.

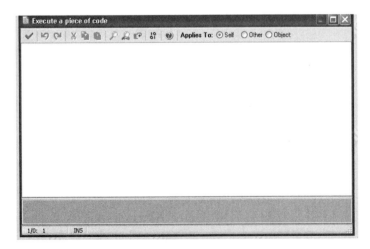

FIGURE D.48   Execute a Piece of Code Property box.

Set the Value of a Variable

This action is used to set the value assigned to a variable. A dialog box titled Set the Value of a Variable opens up when this action is dragged to the Active Actions window as shown in Figure D.49. Four properties need to be defined in this dialog box.

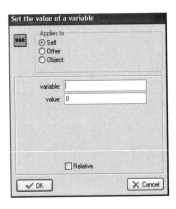

FIGURE D.49   Set the Value of a Variable Property box.

The first editable property consists of three radio buttons labeled Self, Other, and Object. This allows you to apply the current action to either the instance of the object you are working with or to a different instance of some other object. Choosing the radio button labeled Object results in the creation of a new text box as was shown in Figure D.2. This allows you to choose the object to which you would like to apply the current action.

The second editable property, variable, allows the user to type in the variable's name.

The third editable property, value, allows the user to type in the value assigned to the variable.

The last editable property is the checkbox labeled Relative. This field defines whether the value defined is to be added incrementally to its previous value or if the value provided is an absolute value. If the Relative box is checked, the value provided is added to the old value to define the new value. If the Relative box is unchecked, the value provided is the actual value.

If a Variable Has a Value

This action is used to make an appropriate decision based on whether the result of applying a logical operator between the contents of the variable and the supplied value is true or false. A dialog box titled If a Variable Has a Value opens up when this action is dragged to the Active Actions window as shown in Figure D.50. Five properties need to be defined in this dialog box.

The first editable property consists of three radio buttons labeled Self, Other, and Object. This allows you to apply the current action to either the instance of the object you are working with or to a different instance of some other object. Choosing the radio button labeled Object results in the creation of a new text box as was shown in Figure D.2. This allows you to choose the object to which you would like to apply the current action.

The second editable property, variable, allows the user to type in the variable's name.

The third editable property, value, allows the user to type in the value.

The next editable property, operation, allows the user to choose the desired logical operation.

The last editable property is a checkbox labeled Not. It negates the logic used by this action block and executes the next action block only if the result is false.

Put Some Comment

This action is used to add a comment block that typically holds information about the sequence of actions. It is mainly used to help the game creator remember what the sequence of blocks was meant to do. A dialog box titled Put Some Comment opens up when this action is dragged to the Active Actions window as shown in Figure D.51. One property needs to be defined in this dialog box.

The editable property labeled comment allows the user to enter a description of his choice.

FIGURE D.50 If a Variable has a Value Property box.

FIGURE D.51 Put a Comment Property box.

Draw the Value of a Variable

This action is used to draw the value of a variable at a specific location. A dialog box titled Draw the Value of a Variable opens up when this action is dragged to the Active Actions window as shown in Figure D.52. Five properties need to be defined in this dialog box.

The first editable property consists of three radio buttons labeled Self, Other, and Object. This allows you to apply the current action to either the instance of the object you are

FIGURE D.52 Draw the value of a variable Property box.

working with or to a different instance of some other object. Choosing the radio button labeled Object results in the creation of a new text box as was shown in Figure D.2. This allows you to choose the object to which you would like to apply the current action.

The second editable property, variable, allows the user to type in the variable's name.

The third and fourth editable properties, X and Y, allow the user to type in the coordinates where the contents are to be displayed.

The last editable property is the checkbox labeled Relative. This field defines whether the coordinates defined are relative the object's current location or if they define an absolute location.

ACTIONS IN THE SCORE TAB

The actions under found in the Score tab are listed below. A complete description of each of the actions is also provided here.

- Set the Score
- If Score Has a Value
- Draw the Value of a Score
- Show the High Score Table
- Clear the High Score Table
- Set the Number of Lives
- If Lives Is a Value
- Draw the Number of Lives
- Draw the Lives as Image
- Set Health
- If Health Is a Value
- Draw the Health Bar
- Set the Window Caption Info

Set the Score

This action is used to set the score for the game. A dialog box titled Set the Score opens up when this action is dragged to the Active Actions window as shown in Figure D.53. Two properties need to be defined in this dialog box.

The first editable property, new score, is where the value of the new score is to be entered.

The next editable property is the checkbox labeled Relative. This field defines whether the score defined is relative to the object's current score or if it defines the absolute score.

If Score Has a Value

This action is used to make an appropriate decision based on the result of applying a logical operator between the score and the supplied value. A dialog box titled If Score Has a Value opens up when this action is dragged to the Active Actions window as shown in Figure D.54. Three properties need to be defined in this dialog box.

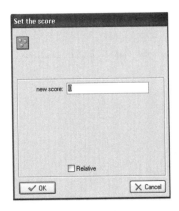

FIGURE D.53   Set the Score Property box.

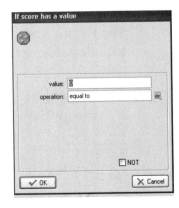

FIGURE D.54   If Score has a Value Property box.

The first editable property, value, allows the user to type in the value the score is to be compared with.

The second editable property, operation, defines the logical operation to perform.

The last editable property is a checkbox labeled Not. It negates the logic used by this action block and executes the next action block only if the result is false.

Draw the Value of a Score

This action is used to draw the value of a score at a specific location. A dialog box titled Draw the Value of a Score opens up when this action is dragged to the Active Actions window as shown in Figure D.55. Four properties need to be defined in this dialog box.

The first and second editable properties, X and Y, determine the location where the score will be displayed.

The third editable property, caption, defines the title to use in front of the score.

The next editable property is the checkbox labeled Relative. This field defines whether the score defined is relative to the object's current score or if is defines the absolute score.

Show the High Score Table

This action is used to display the table that holds all the high scores of the current game. A dialog box titled Show the High Score Table opens up when this action is dragged to the Active Actions window as shown in Figure D.56. Five properties need to be defined in this dialog box.

The five properties define different aspects of the table such as background, border, color, and font.

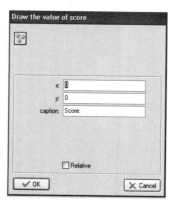

FIGURE D.55 Draw the Value of a Score Property box.

FIGURE D.56 Show the High Score Table Property box.

Clear the High Score Table

This action is used to clear the table that holds all the high scores of the current game.

Set the Number of Lives

This action is used to set the number of lives for the player. A dialog box titled Set the Number of Lives opens up when this action is dragged to the Active Actions window as shown in Figure D.57. Two properties need to be defined in this dialog box.

The first editable property, new lives, is where the number of lives is to be entered.

The next editable property is the checkbox labeled Relative. This field defines whether the lives entered are a relative or an absolute value.

If Lives Is a Value

This action is used to make an appropriate decision based on the result of applying a logical operator between the number of lives and the supplied value. A dialog box titled If Lives Is a Value opens up when this action is dragged to the Active Actions window as shown in Figure D.58. Three properties need to be defined in this dialog box.

FIGURE D.57   Set the Number of Lives Property box.

FIGURE D.58   If Lives is a Value Property box.

The first editable property, value, allows the user to type in the value the lives count is to be compared with.

The second editable property, operation, defines the logical operation to perform.

The last editable property is a checkbox labeled Not. It negates the logic used by this action block and executes the next action block only if the result is false.

Draw the Number of Lives

This action is used to draw the value of a number of lives at a specific location. A dialog box titled Draw the Number of Lives opens up when this action is dragged to the Active Actions window as shown in Figure D.59. Four properties need to be defined in this dialog box.

FIGURE D.59   Draw the Number of Lives Property box.

The first and second editable properties, X and X, determine the location where the lives count will be displayed.

The third editable property, caption, defines the title to use in front of the lives count.

The next editable property is the checkbox labeled Relative. This field defines whether the lives count is a relative or an absolute value.

Draw the Lives as Image

This is similar to the action that displays the lives count except that an image is used to display each life.

Set Health

This action is similar to the Set Score action except that the health is set instead of score.

If Health Is a Value

This action is similar to the If Score Is a Value action except that the health is variable and is checked instead of score.

Draw the Health Bar

This action is similar to the Draw the Score action except that the health is variable and is displayed instead of score. X1 and Y1 define the upper-left corner of the health bar, and X2 and Y2 define the lower-right corner of the health bar.

Set the Window Caption Info

This action is used to selectively display the score, health, and lives. A caption can be specified for each of these variables so that the player knows what these numbers mean when they are displayed.

ACTIONS IN THE DRAW TAB

The actions found in the Draw tab are listed below. A complete description of each of the actions is also provided here.

- Draw a Sprite
- Draw a Background Image
- Draw a Text
- Draw a Text Transformed
- Draw a Rectangle
- Draw a Horizontal Gradient and Draw a Vertical Gradient
- Draw an Ellipse
- Draw a Gradient Ellipse

- Draw Line
- Draw an Arrow
- Set the Color
- Change to Full Screen Mode
- Take a Snapshot Image of the Game
- Create an Effect

The actions listed here are to be used inside a draw event. If they are used elsewhere, they do not exhibit the behavior described.

Draw a Sprite

This action is used to display a sprite at a specific location in the game room. If the sprite is an animated sprite, a subimage number can be specified to display a specific image. The first image of an animated sprite has a value of 0. The default value of −1 draws the current subimage.

Draw a Background Image

This action is used to display a background image that had been earlier loaded as a resource. The tiling option could be used to place multiple copies of the image in the room.

Draw a Text

This action is used to display text at a specific location.

Draw a Text Transformed

This action is also used to display text, but the text can be scaled and rotated as desired. This action is available only in registered versions of Game Maker.

Draw a Rectangle

This action is used to draw a rectangle. The two corners of the rectangle have to be defined.

Draw a Horizontal Gradient and Draw a Vertical Gradient

These two actions also draw a rectangle. The rectangle is filled with a horizontal or vertical gradient. Two colors that create the gradient also need to be specified. This action is available only in registered versions of Game Maker.

Draw an Ellipse

This action is used to draw an ellipse. The two corners of the rectangle enclosing the ellipse have to be specified.

Draw a Gradient Ellipse

This action draws an ellipse and fills it with a gradient. This action is available only in registered versions of Game Maker.

Draw Line

This action draws a line between two specified locations.

Draw an Arrow

This action draws a line between two specified locations with an arrow at the end. The size of the arrow is configurable.

Set the Color

This action is used to set the color for drawing text, lines, and shapes.

Change to Full Screen Mode

This action is used to switch between the full screen and window modes.

Take a Snapshot Image of the Game

This action is used to take a snapshot of the game and store it in a bmp file. This action is available only in registered versions of Game Maker.

Create an Effect

This action is used to create a multitude of different effects such as rain, smoke, clouds, and more.

Index